THE SAN FRANCISCO SHIPPING
CONSPIRACIES OF WORLD WAR ONE

THE SAN FRANCISCO SHIPPING CONSPIRACIES OF WORLD WAR ONE

David H. Grover

WESTERN MARITIME PRESS

ISBN 0-9623935-3-3

TABLE OF CONTENTS

This book is dedicated to the naval and merchant seamen of World War One, who have never received the recognition and respect they deserve for fighting a war whose rules changed with the passing of time.

ACKNOWLEDGMENTS

This account of one of the least gratifying episodes of World War One grew out of the author's earlier efforts to describe the curious circumstances of that war on the west coast of Mexico and the seagoing events of the revolution which was taking place in that country. German ships played a surprisingly active role in those events, particularly the *Leipzig* whose daring departure from Mexican waters has been previously described in several sources. With my curiosity whetted by that earlier research, I set off to learn more about the Germans, whose naval and maritime activities in the Pacific continued to surface as I dug further into the records.

It was then that I first came in contact with James Mossman of Seattle. This diligent scholar had been over much of this interesting ground a number of years ago, had made copious notes, but had never published the results of his work. With his generous cooperation, I was soon delving into the post-*Leipzig* aspects of the German activity: the cases of the *Sacramento* and the *Olson & Mahony*, and the German-Hindu Conspiracy involving the *Annie Larsen* and the *Maverick*. I cannot give enough credit to Jim Mossman for supplying so much documentation of these events, and for steering me to the sources of additional material which I needed in order to learn more of the story. By all rights, his name should appear as co-author on this book, but he has chosen not to accept that designation.

The primary source of material was Record Group 118, Records of U. S. Attorneys and Marshals, preserved at the Pacific-Sierra Regional Center of the National Archives at San Bruno, California. Additional material was acquired from the National Archives in Washington, the Bancroft Library of the University of California, the library of the National Maritime Museum at San Francisco, the Allen Knight Maritime Museum at Monterey, the libraries of the University of California at Berkeley and Davis, the library of the California Maritime Academy, the library of San Jose State University, the library of the Naval Postgraduate School at Monterey, the Naval Historical Center, the Naval War College, the William Jasper Kerr Library of Oregon State University, the Library of Congress, and the Napa Public Library.

Singularly missing from these sources are the thousands of pages of the trial transcripts of the legal cases brought against the defendants. These materials in their original venue were reportedly lost in one of those courthouse fires that have destroyed so many important documents. Copies are said to be available only in Canada and in Europe.

What follows is maritime history. Although the events that were a part of the cargo conspiracies during World War One were sometimes interwoven with other kinds of activities such as espionage and sabotage, I have consciously tried to avoid getting into these matters except insofar as they related directly to the shipping aspects of the conspiracies. This is not to say that these other events were not important; there is simply so much to be said about the ships and the men who operated them that digressions in non-maritime directions would divert attention from the main theme of the book. There are even maritime events with ties to Germany, and in some cases to the Mexican coast as well, which I have ignored because they do not directly impact upon the conspiracies; these include accounts of the schooner "raider" *Alexander Agassiz*, the German gunboat *Geier* that was interned at Honolulu, and the ersatz German consul at Mazatlan whose audacity permitted hundreds of westerners to board ships to escape the revolution.

The story told in the following pages is disillusioning in some respects, in that it reveals a side of American behavior that unduly placed profit over principle. Compounding that disillusionment with the imperfections of individual human behavior is the awareness that the federal government had created the climate in which these individuals pursued their questionable profits.

This is a story that desperately cries out for a hero, but, unfortunately, no one answers that call.

CHAPTER ONE

NEUTRALITY AND THE NAVY

Early in World War One the Pacific coast of North America became the arena for a strange series of maritime dramas. These events were replete with the kind of intrigue and mystery that can readily transform the established facts of history into high adventure. They included threats to commerce posed by German surface raiders, the use of remote neutral harbors by German warships and their merchant auxiliaries, and the efforts of incongruous conspiracies that were established to utilize merchant ships of the United States in supplying German warships and causes.

As the war moved toward its ultimate resolution, these unusual events became increasingly scarce; consequently, they should be regarded as products of American neutrality, more so than of the nation's limited period of belligerency during the war. It is entirely possible that neutrality itself became a sort of catalyst for many of the unusual events that were to occur in the eastern Pacific Ocean during the first part of the war. These events often seemed to grow out of ambiguities that the so-called rules of neutrality which were then in existence were incapable of resolving.

In 1914 neutrality was a new and perhaps confusing idea for Americans. In earlier times, the posture of neutrality in warfare had been relatively easy to recognize whenever it had been adopted by a nation at a particular point in history. However, the notion of neutrality as an abstract philosophical concept or as a legal commitment were sometimes difficult for pragmatic people such as Americans to understand; furthermore, efforts by the "experts" to explain, analyze, or rationalize this international proclamation of non-partisanship in actual practice were often misunderstood.

Americans had always enjoyed distance as an automatic means of avoiding entanglement in European conflicts. In 1914, however, distance had ceased to be a guarantee of peaceful isolation, as most of the leading nations of the world had established colonies in Africa, Asia, and Oceania which represented new frontiers for potential conflict. In a new role as a world power, the United States for the first time had to accept the responsibility of deciding whether to join alliances engaged in foreign wars or to remain neutral—whatever that might entail.

Fortunately, a set of guidelines for making such decisions and for behaving properly as either a belligerent or neutral was evolving at this time. At the turn of the century, Europe, along with a hiatus from continental wars, was enjoying an intellectual ferment which sought to rationalize human behavior in all sorts of activities, including war. This was the era of the great conferences among nations which set out to civilize warfare: the Hague Conventions in 1899 and 1907 and the Declaration of London of 1909. Not only did belligerents get considerable attention in these international pacts, but neutrals also found their rights and responsibilities spelled out. Warfare at sea as well as on land, together with the rudiments of aerial warfare, were given considerable attention in both the rules for belligerents and for neutrals.

Translating the theoretical and quasi-contractual aspects of these concepts into practice, however, could be difficult for those nations that adopted the policy of neutrality. This book will concern itself with how the first World War, particularly that portion of the war in which the United States remained neutral, gave rise to a series of shipping conspiracies and frauds which brought discredit to a number of Americans, and embarrassment to the government. While these events took place on both coasts of the United States, it was on the west coast that the frauds attained their most diverse and innovative nature. In the pages that follow, the most significant of these cases will be reviewed from their origin to their resolution.

In 1914 Americans were admittedly naive about power politics at the international level. In fact, that era has sometimes been called the nation's "age of innocence." In initially electing to remain uncommitted to either side in the developing war, the United States faced several difficult challenges for which it was not adequately prepared. The first was to display exemplary behavior as the leading neutral nation of the world, a responsibility on which the country initially stumbled badly. The second challenge was subsequently to throw off the numbing effects of that neutrality in order to fight a war in which most of the enemy's forces had been already driven from the sea, leaving only a few residual threats which were frequently more embarrassing than menacing, at least in the Pacific Ocean. Adding to the frustration of the United States in pursuing, before later abandoning, neutrality was the fact that, although the early problems introduced by neutrality were often linked to naval operations, they were generally not the kinds of issues to which the United States Navy could bring much expertise or insight, much less any corrective action.

Shortly after the start of the war, inconsistencies in the way the newly-codified rules of neutrality were interpreted in the United States sent a series of dangerous false signals to American entrepreneurs in the marine shipping industry. This uneven interpretation encouraged certain American citizens to engage in activities, many of which the authorities had, rather unwisely, approved as being appropriate and proper within the principles of neutrality, but which were later determined to be criminal violations of the neutral status of the country. As a result of the latter determinations, a number of the perpetrators, if that is the correct word for people who believed they had the blessing of their government in doing what they did, were sent to prison and/or fined. The American civilian officials who brought the legal actions against these people quite possibly were guilty of initially under-reacting to the ambiguities in the law that entrapped so many people, and then over-reacting when they discovered how gullible their own responses had been at the outset.

In all fairness to these inept officials, however, it should be noted that most of the Americans who were caught up in these scandals were motivated by the prospect of high profits, a situation usually accompanied by high risks. Furthermore, many of these aggressive businessmen and opportunists had shown themselves willing to make declarations to their government which they knew to be false in order to achieve those profits.

Most of these troubling events took place during the opening year of the World War. The broad arena was the Pacific coast of North and South America, with the specific transactions of these notorious cases occurring largely within the shipping community of the port of San Francisco, one of the most cosmopolitan, romantic, and glamorous cities of the world. The players in this strange drama came from all walks of life: aristocratic German diplomats, American shipping officials, merchant officers and seamen, Hindu nationalists, American government and corporate bureaucrats, small business owners, lawyers, et al. Perhaps the greatest surprise in the court cases that developed from these events was the degree to which responsible middle-class native-born American businessmen were found guilty of various crimes against the federal government in trying to aid Germany—for a profit.

The documents which preserve the record of the neutrality frauds of 1914-15 unfortunately do a much better job of describing the workings and enforcement of the laws than they do the feelings of the people who were caught up by the imperfections of those laws. Neither the court documents nor newspaper accounts capture much of the human drama inherent in such cases. Only a few photographs of the defendants appeared in the newspapers, and no accounts of their careers. Inasmuch as some of these cases did not come to trial until after the United States had entered the Great War, the lack of such information could be attributed to the pseudo-secrecy imposed by wartime conditions, but initially, before the constraints of national security intervened, the press seems to have done an inadequate job of exploring how so many seemingly solid citizens could get into such trouble.

Even though the general tenor of these conspiracies was disillusioning to the public, there was significant human courage and heroism displayed in the course of the events that unfolded during these questionable transactions. Nonetheless, no one person emerged from this milieu as a genuine hero, or even as a leading historical figure. Instead, Americans caught glimpses of a number of men on both sides of the conflict whose conduct under difficult conditions was worthy of admiration and respect, and whose dedication to their respective causes was commendable. There were also, of course, a few thoroughly unlikable men appearing as players in the strange drama.

Only a half dozen ships and their operators were directly involved in the neutrality frauds on the west coast of the United States. Two of these vessels were under the Mexican flag, the steamers *Mazatlan* and *Marie*; these ships carried American coal to the German cruiser *Leipzig* off South America by way of trans-shipment at Guaymas, Mexico. Another was the German freighter *Alexandria* which was re-flagged as the American *Sacramento* before carrying coal to a German cruiser squadron in the same area. Still another was the *Olson & Mahony*, a ship belonging to the American steamship company of that same name, which was attempting to replicate the *Sacramento*'s trip, but was prevented from doing so by American authorities. The other two vessels were the *Maverick*, an American ship acquired by German interests, and the *Annie Larsen*, a schooner belonging to the Olson and Mahony firm; these two ships were involved in a gun-running venture which went awry. Dozens of Californians, including some who thought they were doing no wrong, were parties to the lies and deceit which characterized the operations of these six ships, and many of these people eventually paid the price for their duplicity.

Several other American-flag vessels were also involved in this story in a less direct way. These include the schooners *Henry S.* and *Alexander Agassiz*, and the steamers *Minnesotan* and *Rio Pasig*. Peripheral as their roles might have been, these vessels knowingly served the German cause to some degree.

If it seems strange to speak of ships as "knowingly" serving a cause, or in having intentions, behavior, or personal attributes, the usage in attaching such human traits to these inanimate structures of steel and wood is legitimized by the practice in law of treating ships as individuals having rights and responsibilities just as people do. Men, of course, direct the movements of ships—subject to occasional intervention by nature—so it should be understood that when a ship is described as having taken a course of action, it is the captain of the ship who has acted. Nevertheless, a ship does sometimes acquire a personality and perhaps even a personification, making it perfectly natural to think of the vessel as a being. The use of the pronoun *she* in lieu of the neutral and neutered *it* in describing a vessel is part of the same general feeling. Thus, as with the people in this story, there may be some heroic ships to be encountered ahead, and possibly even a villain or two.

Americans who recall the nation's neutrality during the first two years of World War II may have a difficult time understanding how the neutrality of the first 30 months of World War I differed from the anti-Nazi neutrality of 1940-41. In 1914 the experience of immigration from Europe was fresher in the memories of many Americans than in later years, as was the distasteful recollection of the intrigue and political maneuvering of the Great Powers in Europe. Furthermore, there was no clear-cut dichotomy between the good guys of Europe and the bad guys; the British and French could be as exasperating to Americans as could the Germans or Russians.

In the past, Americans sometimes had been given reason to distrust "perfidious Albion." The United States had fought two wars against Great Britain, including one of independence, and had encountered pro-Confederacy sympathies from that country during a third war. However, the strong political, cultural, and linguistic ties which Americans had maintained with Great Britain through the years generally overcame any residual hostility from the past, except, perhaps, for German-Americans and Irish-Americans.

No events or personalities had contributed to any intrinsic antipathy toward things or people German. In fact, the opposite was true. German culture was much admired; the language was taught extensively in public schools, and German contributions to the sciences, the arts, and the humanities were widely recognized. Some fifty-five German-language newspapers were published in the United States at that time, including one in San Francisco. As Mark Sullivan pointed out in his monumental *Our Times*, "The natural disposition of America was to think well of Germany. Had any one on August 3, 1914, or a week or a month or a year before, said to a group in a cigar store that in any European war, with Germany on one side and France and Russia on the other (as the line-up stood on August 3,) America would participate, he would have been jeered at."[1]

At the outset of the war the Germans, like the British, were regarded as a highly civilized people with whom the United States had no quarrel. To many Americans, England and Germany seemed like cousins in the family of nations, just as their sovereigns were indeed cousins. At least initially, the war may have appeared to be a family fight. Consequently, the climate of neutrality in the United States in 1914 was considerably more tolerant and impartial than that which developed later when Germany's conduct of the war became more brutal, or that which was to prevail during the early days of World War II. What all of this meant was that sympathy toward or even assistance to the German cause was not unusual among Americans early in the war, and worldly San Franciscans were no exception.

Under the rules of neutrality as codified in the Hague Convention of 1907 merchant ships were treated quite differently from warships. While a warship of a belligerent nation was subject to internment if it entered a neutral port and remained longer than the 24 hours allowed for fueling or effecting repairs, merchant ships of belligerent nations were not normally subject to internment. In fact, the rules were predicated on the assumption that trade would continue to flow throughout a war, and that, not only could neutrals trade with each other, neutral ships could trade with belligerents and belligerent ships could trade with neutrals. In all cases the ships were subject to search and seizure to determine if the cargo were contraband, a provision later abandoned by the belligerents when unrestricted submarine warfare developed. Consequently, merchant ships of belligerent nations could enter neutral ports, provided that they did nothing there (including the loading of contraband cargo) that would prejudice the neutrality of the host nation, and provided that they were willing to assume any risks that might result from their departure. As a result of worldwide British naval superiority, many German ships found refuge in neutral ports during the early days of the World War, and stayed there rather than risking capture in trying to continue to trade.[2]

The rules under which neutrals could trade were at worst contradictory, and at best subject to differing interpretations. For example, the Hague Convention of 1907 said in Article 6 that "The supply, in any manner, directly or indirectly, by a neutral Power to a belligerent Power, of war-ships, ammunition, or war material of any kind whatever, is forbidden." However, the very next paragraph, Article 7, said that "A neutral Power is not bound to prevent the export or transit, for the use of either belligerent, of arms, ammunition, or, in general, of anything which could be of use to an army or fleet." Thus, one article appeared to prohibit any trading with a belligerent in war material, while the other said that neutrals were not required to prevent the trade in such material.

Even greater ambiguities existed with respect to what constituted contraband which neutrals were forbidden to carry in their ships. Munitions were clearly contraband (although

Article 7 appeared to say that neutrals could trade in such commodities) but many types of cargoes were conditionally contraband, depending upon the use to which the item in question was put. Food was the classic example; food for fighting men was contraband, but food for the civilians of a belligerent country was not, with the captain of a naval vessel that stopped a merchant ship on the high seas with such a cargo on board having to decide which was which. Fuel was another example of conditional contraband. As might be expected, there was wide disagreement among the experts on international law concerning the interpretation of these so-called principles of neutrality.

The enforcement of neutrality laws at sea presumes a capability for boarding and inspecting vessels at sea. This responsibility generally fell to the U. S. Navy, although the Revenue Cutter Service, which merged with the Lifesaving Service in 1915 to form the U. S. Coast Guard, theoretically should have played a stronger role in this enforcement responsibility. It would be unwise to assume, however, that the Navy in World War One was heavily involved with neutrality enforcement. The Pacific Fleet, long a stepchild of the Navy, had neither the modern ships nor the personnel to do a thorough job of screening the many merchant ships that were moving cargoes to and from west coast ports under the inducement of the high freight rates that prevailed in wartime.

The Navy frequently seemed to be unsure of itself, and to be unable to provide the right ship in the right place at the right time. This problem within the naval forces based in California was part of a larger problem of a U. S. Navy experiencing extensive change. At the turn of the century the Navy had briefly enjoyed a respite from the Spanish American War, a two-front war which had taxed its capabilities even though the enemy, particularly at Manila Bay, was weak and inept. Considerable postwar expansion to the fleet then began in the early 1900s as Americans, under the impetus of the ideas of Alfred A. Mahan as popularized by Theodore Roosevelt, accepted the proposition that the United States, now a world power with insular possessions, should have a Navy second only to Great Britain. Much of the expansion occurred, however, through the development of battleships, a vessel type which would have only limited value in the offshore patrols that were required up and down the coasts of the American continents.

The concept of a fleet as a formal naval entity had previously existed only in the Atlantic; elsewhere, there were two less comprehensive organizations in existence: the Pacific Squadron in the eastern Pacific, and the Asiatic Squadron which had been responsible for the easy victory at Manila Bay. Although the distances involved in fighting the Spanish-American War, both in Cuba and the Philippines, had required a makeshift call-up of a number of merchant ships to serve as transports, supply ships, and even combatants, little had been done after that war to give to the Navy any degree of self-sufficiency for operations away from stateside home bases. Along with a shortage of ships of the train, the lack of bases and coaling stations also limited such operations.[3]

The Pacific Squadron was reorganized at the beginning of 1907 to give it several divisions of cruisers. Within a few months the Pacific Fleet was formally established with two squadrons of cruisers, including several of the newer armored cruisers as well as a few of the older protected cruisers. There were also several flotilla of destroyers and the older torpedo boats within the new fleet, but these early vessels had limited all-weather capability. During the battleship-oriented Roosevelt presidency, few small vessels of sturdy construction were built; consequently, the kind of rugged modern gunboat which was to be needed along the North American coastline to fight brushfires and enforce neutrality during the first two decades of the 20th century simply did not exist.

Under the leadership of George von Lengerke Meyer, President Taft's highly regarded Secretary of the Navy, a needed system of maintenance and the rotation of vessels was established. A number of older vessels were laid up in the Pacific Reserve Fleet at Bremerton, including the old battleship *Oregon*, a half dozen cruisers of various types, a few torpedo boats, two submarines, and a submarine tender. These ships rotated to sea duty periodically, with personnel being shifted from vessel to vessel to make these sea tours possible as well as to keep the men trained.

After the opening of the Panama Canal in August, 1914, ships could be transferred back and forth between oceans. However, the events at Vera Cruz earlier that year required a fleet-size American naval presence on the east coast of Mexico, and after the United States entered the World War in 1917 all available ships were needed in the Atlantic. Consequently, the flow of warships between oceans was decidedly from Pacific to Atlantic during the first four years of the operation of the canal. As a result, the number of ships on the west coast at any time was considerably smaller than the total number of ships officially designated as components of the Pacific fleet.

Administratively, the Pacific Fleet went through several changes during the early days of World War I. In mid-1915 it was given four-star status, with Admiral Thomas B. Howard the first beneficiary of the higher rank. Nothing else was made commensurate with the rank, however; at one point Howard had only one old armored cruiser in his fleet. The reserve fleet at Bremerton had additional ships, of course, but personnel and budget shortages had left these ships inadequately maintained. Nevertheless, the head of this fleet, Rear Admiral William F. Fullam who had just left a prestigious post as superintendent of the Naval Academy, labored diligently to get these ships ready for service.

In 1916 the Navy Department authorized the use of the Pacific Reserve Fleet vessels on active duty, but without placing them in full commission or treating them as units of the Pacific fleet. Soon an awkward situation developed as the Commander of the Reserve Fleet and the Commander of the Pacific Fleet both felt that they should have operational control over the ships. Admiral Fullam of the Reserve Fleet seems to have won out on this issue, largely because he stayed in the billet for several years, while the Pacific Fleet billet changed frequently with Admirals Howard, Winslow, and Caperton occupying it successively during the years of the World War.

Frequent administrative changes continued, affecting the way that the ships on the west coast of the United States were utilized. In May, 1917, the Pacific Reserve Fleet was abolished, becoming instead Patrol Force, Pacific Fleet. This would have been an accurate and meaningful designation for the ships that were patrolling in Mexico and along the coast, but in reality the unit became a cruiser patrol force that was immediately shifted to the Atlantic Ocean under Admiral William B. Caperton. Subsequently, two months later the coastal ships were re-designated Division Two, Pacific Fleet, and that designation was retained for the balance of the war with Rear Admiral Fullam serving as the *de facto* commander of naval forces in the eastern Pacific.

As a result of all this change, early in the World War on the west coast the United States found itself trying to police the doctrine of neutrality which was a new and troublesome public policy with a Navy that was going through technological and administrative change while it was also short of ships, men, and experience. These circumstances created an open invitation for aggressive and resourceful individuals, German and American, who were prepared to challenge the system.

The first section of this book will explore several of the more significant efforts to test the American response to the ambiguities of neutrality, along with the tardy but harsh reactions made by United States officials to those efforts. If the United States Navy seems singularly absent from several of these transactions, this situation can be attributed to two factors: the Navy's preoccupation with the heavy commitment of warships to the Gulf of California in protecting American interests during the Mexican revolution, and its intelligence organization which seemed to be several jumps behind the Germans in the game of intrigue.

Subsequent sections of the book will consider the responses of the United States government to the neutrality violations, including some of the events of the year-and-a-half of American participation in the war in the Pacific. The treatment of those latter years will culminate with a look at the outcomes for the conspirators, those people who had been enticed into unwise and mercenary partisanship by the nation's muddled interpretation of its own neutrality laws.

During these final sticky episodes the Navy was aware, and perhaps even grateful, that much of the bizarre naval war in the eastern Pacific was being waged ashore by the criminal justice system and other branches of the federal government. It had not been a war of which a military service could be terribly proud, nor one which left behind memories of heroic American men and ships who had acted as what would today be called role models. Instead, the war on the west coast was a grubby backwater of a larger war. That larger war may have been fought over matters of principle in the trenches of Europe and on the North Atlantic, but, on the western shores of the Americas, principle frequently gave way to expediency.

In that setting, driven by self-serving motives, a number of unprincipled people came onto the scene, some of whom were likely candidates for membership in a conspiracy that was soon to emerge from the confusion of the neutrality laws.

CHAPTER TWO

GERMAN RAIDERS: A FIRST TASTE

The German-American cargo conspiracies of 1914-15 have their roots in the actions of a German cruiser which left Mexican waters for a brief career as a surface raider before joining a squadron of cruisers. Without this ship, there would have been no need for the logistics efforts that spawned the questionable conduct that took place within the San Francisco shipping community.

Perhaps no aspect of naval warfare has survived into the 20th century with so much mystery and romance surrounding it as has the notion of surface raiders. Although a bit of this lore survived into the Second World War, World War I represented the zenith of this tradition, as well as the beginning of a rapid decline. The preeminence of the raider early in that war reflected the existence of a number of easy victims such as sailing ships and ships without radios, together with the absence of widespread aerial reconnaissance and any electronic surveillance. It also reflected the reality that the potential of the submarine as an offensive weapon had not yet been fully realized by the navies of the world, at least not in 1914.

The nation that embraced the concept of the sea raider more completely than all others was Germany. The sinister appellation of *Hun* that had been widely applied to the Germans at the time certainly carried the connotation of a raider, although this usage was etiologically incorrect since it was the Goths who were the Germanic raiders and not the Huns who were Asians. It was also inaccurate in a maritime sense in that neither the Huns nor Goths were ocean raiders. Consequently, as a continental power the Germans were late in discovering the benefits of sea raiding; they had no tradition of the privateer on which to build, as did the English, French, Dutch, and Americans. But when Germany first achieved nationhood and became a worldwide maritime and naval power in the latter part of the 19th century, her leaders soon recognized that raiding would fit uniquely into the nation's naval strategy.

Boxed into a narrow coastline on the North Sea and the Baltic, Germany understood, perhaps better than any other modern naval power, how important it was for her surface ships, both naval and merchant, to be able to break out of blockades at home and at her foreign outposts, avoid detection, and harass the enemy. During the years prior to the war as they looked ahead to the conflict they knew was coming, German military planners saw an opportunity to make raiding a planned part of naval operations, not just a spur-of-the-moment improvisation. Tactics and logistics were developed carefully, and plans made for the needed ships and bases. As John Philips Cranwell notes in a history of raiding in the age of steam, ". . . plans were drawn up to use freighters to carry coal, food, and ammunition to appointed rendezvous or to raiders. Commerce destroyers, once at sea, would not have to put into a neutral port for anything."[1]

It is unlikely that German naval planners ever believed that raiders would enjoy this degree of independence, but the early experience of the German raiders would soon demonstrate that with resourcefulness and luck, a raider captain might go unreported for months at a time during which he could inflict significant damage to shipping, particularly if he could keep a collier close by.

A number of books have been written about the exploits of the daring German captains who commanded the well-known raiders of World War I. The names of these men—von Müller, zu Dohna, von Luckner, Nerger—conjure up images of aristocratic and dedicated captains who were nevertheless decent human beings. These men soon became popular legends; it is quite likely that there have been as many admirers of these ships and their captains among those who were enemies of Germany as there have been among the German people. Perhaps it was the highly civilized behavior of the raider captains, as well as their courage and resourcefulness, that made them the heroes they have become.

Regardless of the skills of the captains, the stealth of the surface raiders could not have been maintained without occasional visits to harbors in which the ships and their crews were able to renew themselves with physical resources such as food, water, and fuel, and psychological resources such as rest. While it was not a central arena of World War I, the west coast of Mexico provided a number of hidden harbors which were ideal for supporting the covert activities of such ships. As one of the very first of the raiders of World War I, the German cruiser *Leipzig* operated briefly from these harbors.

In the United States, military thinking in 1914 still had plenty of room to accommodate fanciful notions about surface raiders preying on ocean commerce, and even attacking American ports. The Endicott Board Report of 1885 had given impetus to the development of an elaborate system of harbor defense in the United States, much of it predicated on the assumption that surface raiders could indeed attack the ports of the East, Gulf, or West coasts, as well as prey upon our ocean commerce. That report still dominated military planning prior to World War I. Before the United States entered the war, the Coast Artillery component of the Army remained one of the most influential branches of service. However, within the Navy (which had never been as enthusiastic as had the Army about coast defense), the torpedo boats which were originally conceived by the Endicott Report as harbor defense vessels had been displaced by torpedo boat destroyers.[2]

Perhaps this latter development was a fortunate one in combatting the threat of raiders, in that such predatory ships, if they did exist, would likely have to be ferreted out of their lairs by opposing navies, rather than be destroyed by coast artilleryman simply waiting for these ships to come under the range of coast defense batteries if they tried to enter American harbors. A few of the early destroyers were sent to the Gulf of California as a part of the American naval presence on the Mexican coast during the revolution in that country and the early days of the World War,[3] but they were utilized rather timidly and did not challenge merchant vessels at sea.

Prior to 1910 the United States had enjoyed comfortable relations with Mexico during the long tenure of Porfirio Diaz as president of that country. Following the start of the Mexican revolution, however, came a decade of distrust and suspicion. At the outset of World War One, Germany which had developed a strong presence and influence in Mexico was quick to capitalize on any friction between the two countries in the expectation that if the United States were forced to maintain large troop strength on the border, such troops would not be available to be sent to Europe, thus keeping America out of the war.

Two American interventions into Mexico contributed significantly to the bad feeling, and in each case German complicity compounded the ill will on both sides. One was at

Vera Cruz where a large Navy and Marine landing force was put ashore in 1914 in response to what had originally been only a diplomatic slight; this intervention soon turned into a naval blockade to prevent German ships from delivering cargoes of arms and ammunition to Mexican forces. The second incursion was the 1916 punitive expedition deep into Mexico in pursuit of Pancho Villa, a beneficiary of German arms shipments, who announced during the campaign that he was going "to help the Germans whip the United States and obtain Texas, Arizona, and California back for Mexico."[4]

Although American land forces were swallowed up and ineffective in the interior of Mexico, the U. S. Navy could easily dominate the coastline of Mexico from bases in the Caribbean and in southern California. Mexico was of no consequence as a naval power, but she had something that other navies coveted: the magnificent inlets on the west coast of the country: Magdalena Bay, Turtle Bay, and Whale Bay. Although they lacked port facilities and land-based transportation, these bays were expansive and deep, and, best of all, isolated from prying eyes. Consequently, if there were to be raiders on the Pacific Coast in the First World War, there were no better sites from which to operate than these lonely bays in Mexico.

Germany had twice tried to buy Magdalena Bay as a naval base from the American company which owned the land around it. The first of these attempts had occurred in 1903 but was thwarted when pressure from the United States caused the Kaiser to back away. Again in 1914 Germany made a strong push to acquire the area, but when the arrangements were finally in place, the outbreak of the war intervened.[5] Germany was not alone in seeking this area for a base; both Japan and the United States had made similar efforts.

Unquestionably, there *were* German raiders active in the Pacific Ocean at various times during World War One. At the outset, the German cruiser *Leipzig* was such a ship. Perhaps better than the actions of any other ship in the eastern Pacific, her movements along the northwest coast of Mexico personified the image of a clandestine raider utilizing equally clandestine anchorages. In fact, within one month she visited at least three of the hidden harbors of Baja California. Although her wartime tenure on the west coast of Mexico was brief, she was able to conjure up all the shadowy images of raiders rendezvousing with mother ships in secret locations before venturing out to prey upon commerce.[6]

SMS (Sein Majestäts Schiff) *Leipzig* was one of a number of lightly-armored cruisers built in Germany early in the century. These ships of about 340 feet in length and drawing only about 18 feet were suitable for, if not actually intended for, raiding. In the summer of 1914 the *Leipzig* had only recently relieved the cruiser *Nürnberg* as the German station ship at Mazatlan, on the Mexican mainland near the broad mouth of the Gulf of California. The need to evacuate foreign nationals from revolution-torn Mexico had brought warships of several nations into this area. For the most part, serving aboard these cruisers in Mexican waters was considered pleasant duty by the crew, particularly during the winter months when the heat was not oppressive. The only operational movements for the *Leipzig* were occasional trips to other coastal locations to pick up German nationals seeking refuge from the uncertainties of the revolution.

The captains of the men-of-war of several other nations which anchored regularly in the harbor had similar responsibilities, and these commanding officers developed a bond of friendship and mutual respect. In fact, at the end of July, 1914, the evacuation of foreigners from Mazatlan was carried out jointly by the crews of the German, British, and American warships, with the cooperation of representatives of both the federal and rebel troops which were at that moment contesting for the city. The niceties of military courtesy were still observed, with warships firing salutes to the men-of-war of other nations as well as to both factions in the revolution.

But it was the World War, not the revolution, that created the crisis for the *Leipzig*. On August 2, 1914, just hours before the outbreak of the war, the American cruiser at Mazatlan, the USS *California*, received coded radio messages to be forwarded to the warships of the European powers which were present in the harbor, the *Leipzig* under the German flag and the Canadian sloop *Algerine* representing the United Kingdom. These messages had been sent through the receiver of the *California* because she had the most dependable electronic communication in the area via her direct link to the Navy's powerful radio station at San Diego. (The Canadian ship, a veteran of the Bering Sea Patrol, did not even have electricity, much less radio.) These messages apparently alerted each ship to the imminent onset of hostilities, which meant that the warships of those nations which were going to war could no longer stay in neutral waters without the risk of internment.[7]

The *Leipzig* in recent days had collected 35 German and British nationals who were refugees from the hostilities of the revolution. After delivering this human cargo to the safety of the *California*, the German cruiser stood out to sea. While this was happening, the Canadian gunboat delivered her refugees to the *California*. She also coaled from the USS *Saturn*; this largesse was through the courtesy of Admiral Thomas B. Howard, USN, who flew his flag as Commander in Chief, Pacific Fleet, from the halyards of the *California*. Inasmuch as war had not yet been declared, this assistance represented no violation of American neutrality. Furthermore, the coaling gave the diminutive Canadian ship additional hours in port, delaying her departure an appropriate interval of time so as to minimize the chances of her encountering the much larger *Leipzig* at sea.

Subsequently, the *Algerine* headed for home waters to the north as quickly as possible, a passage which must have been full of tense moments for the men aboard, operating in wartime with no radio. Perhaps it was just as well that were unable to know that the officers and men of the *Leipzig*, until recently their friends but now adversaries, would keep their ship on the coast of Mexico and California for several more weeks.[8] Through the ensuing years there has been speculation that the friendship between the two crews was responsible for the *Leipzig* allowing the relatively harmless Canadian ship to sail north unmolested.

After leaving Mazatlan, the *Leipzig* sailed north along the Mexican coast. On August 3, off Cabo San Lucas, she encountered and exchanged radio messages with the Hamburg American Line freighter *Alexandria*, bound for San Francisco under charter to the Kosmos Line. According to the official German naval history of World War I, the *Leipzig* ordered the freighter to proceed to San Francisco as a supply ship as rapidly as possible, and there to load 5,000 tons of coal and 2,000 kilograms of machine oil for the cruiser. She also sent an order ahead to the German shore staff in San Francisco for 8,000 tons of coal and as much grease as obtainable, to meet her own needs and those of other German ships, and dispatched her supply officer, Dr. Simon Reimer, aboard the *Alexandria* to insure that the supplies were obtained. The radio message also alluded to ships in San Francisco Bay that were then being readied to go to Saipan, not far from Pagan Island where the German Far East fleet had gone upon the outbreak of the war.[9]

On August 5 the *Leipzig* entered the broad confines of Magdalena Bay on the Pacific Coast of Baja where she then coaled from a British ship, the *Cetriana*, which had been at Mazatlan under a charter drawn up originally by the German consulate in San Francisco in behalf of the *Nürnberg*. As a part of the charter the Germans had put aboard the ship a radio set, as well as their own operator; consequently the merchant captain's knowledge of world events including the impending war was limited to what his radio operator told him. This freighter under the command of LT E. J. Minister, RNR, was already a veteran of the hostilities spawned by the revolution, having evacuated foreigners under hostile fire from Mexico earlier in 1914.[10] Now, at Magdalena Bay even though the World War had been declared the previous day and he was therefore entitled to seize or sink his collier because she flew the distinctive blue ensign of the British Naval Reserve, Captain Haun of the *Leipzig* gallantly let the merchant ship go free after removing her radio. Although he received little of the acclaim bestowed on other raider captains, Johannes Haun was every bit a part of their tradition of chivalry.

After coaling at Magdalena, the *Leipzig* slowly worked her way north, without any contact with shipping. Although the ship generally stayed out of the steamer track, there was a general hope aboard that she might stumble upon an "*Empress*" steamer which could be captured. That expectation may have been unrealistic, however, in that the Canadian Pacific steamers normally were not found in the coastal trade off Mexico.

The cruiser looked for but did not find the Mexican island of Guadalupe, where she reportedly expected to find a steamer assigned to her. When a report reached the ship that the *Alexandria* had stopped at San Diego because she was on fire and that she was being guarded by the *Algerine*, the *Leipzig* at dawn on the 8th, apparently undetected, cruised past San Diego and scanned the bay which was clearly visible across the sand spit at Coronado. When no evidence of the German ship or any enemy ship was seen, the cruiser proceeded north. On the 11th the *Leipzig* was off the Farallon Islands, outside the Golden Gate, where she was first detected by American naval vessels, the armored cruisers *South Dakota* and *Pittsburg*.[11]

When the presence of the German cruiser outside the Golden Gate was announced in the press, there was widespread anticipation that a major battle might develop between this ship and one of the British cruisers. In fact, crowds of people assembled on high ground on the Marin headlands overlooking the ocean at the entrance to the bay, hoping to witness such a battle.

The British believed that the German cruiser had been lurking outside San Francisco with the *Nürnberg*, an erroneous assumption which the Germans did nothing to correct. Some reports indicated that during the time she was unaccounted for the *Leipzig* had gone up the coast as far as British Columbia; in reality, she went north only as far as Cape Mendocino, and this trip was made after her presence outside the bay was already known. Apparently, the cruiser was prepared to take on the Canadian cruiser *Rainbow* had she found her on this scouting deployment, but she found no enemy ships.

Originally, the Germans had hoped to avoid forcing the *Leipzig* to enter port by coaling her at sea off San Francisco from a barge brought out by a tugboat. The barge to be utilized was actually an old American barque that was engaged by a motion picture production company in filming movies outside the bay, a circumstance that prompted newspapermen to report the arrangement as an imaginative way to fuel ships offshore secretly on a regular basis if the Germans had been so inclined. Soon, however, officials at the German consulate abandoned the arrangements for the coaling at sea when they learned how difficult that operation might become.

In the meantime, however, arrangements for fuel had been made by Dr. Simon Reimer, the supply officer of the *Leipzig* who had arrived on the freighter *Alexandria*. These arrangements included the purchase of 500 tons of sacked coal for the offshore fueling operation from the brokerage firm of Rothschild & Company for $5,000, with the coal supplied by Western Fuel Company. After the cancellation of the offshore operation, Reimer then purchased additional bulk coal from the same source with funds supplied by the consulate. There was also about 2,000 tons of Navy coal set aside for the *Leipzig* by previous arrangement at the Mare Island shipyard; the *Cetriana* had drawn upon this supply in coaling the cruiser in Mexico. However, the U. S. Navy indicated that it could not make this coal available to the cruiser after the outbreak of hostilities.

In aborting the offshore coaling, the Germans at the consulate drew upon the experience they had recently gained in making a visit to the *Leipzig* out beyond the Farallons. On August 12, the tug *Active*, under charter from the Hearst newspaper, the *Examiner*, went out to the cruiser which was about five miles north of the Farallons. En route, the party, which included, in addition to two reporters, the German vice consul E. F. von Schack and a person identified as his secretary, stopped for lunch aboard the pilot boat with which the cruiser had been in regular contact. The extra person aboard the tug was later identified by the consul as Dr. Reimer. After the rendezvous with the *Leipzig*, the tug returned to the bay with two sick German sailors who were to be hospitalized.[12]

The reporters, of course, brought back the fruits of their labor—an interview with Captain Haun. The wide-ranging interview indicated that the cruiser had destroyed all her boats in order to be stripped for action, that she was regularly in touch with the *Nürnberg* which was hovering outside the port (which was not true), and that the officers were confident that the cruiser could dispose of opposing warships at the rate of one a day. Rear Admiral Charles Pond, commandant of the 12th Naval District, condemned the newspaper's action in sending out the tugboat, calling it "unneutral service and a violation of the President's proclamation of neutrality" because the resultant news stories revealed the location and movements of a belligerent vessel.[13] This criticism was nullified, however, by the cruiser's ongoing contact with the pilot boat which had resulted in her presence being reported in shipping news, and by her subsequent entry into the port which became a matter of public record all over the world.

The cruiser finally entered the bay on August 17. During the 24-hour visit which she was permitted under international law, the *Leipzig* while at anchor was able to obtain a partial load of bunker coal from the bulk supply obtained by Reimer, enough to enable her to reach the closest German port-of-call in

Samoa, with the understanding that en route she could make another coaling stop in Honolulu. She also managed to ship additional personnel, with an number of men from the *Alexandria* and the *Serapis*, another Kosmos Line ship, joining her crew, along with nine men who were recruited ashore, the latter action representing a clear-cut violation of the Hague Convention.[14]

Even though all hands were utilized in the process, coaling a man of war was a laborious, lengthy, and dirty process, made more difficult by the small size of the scuttles and chutes through which the coal was moved, a requirement imposed by the need to preserve the watertight integrity of the hull of the ship. The speed with which the task was accomplished was also dependent upon the facilities at which it was carried out. Coaling at a shore base with a tipple that could gravitate coal into the ship was obviously faster than coaling from a regular barge alongside from which the coal had to be lifted aboard. Both procedures were infinitely easier, however, than coaling at sea which required the two ships to be lashed together, risking damage to their hull plates and superstructure as the swells banged them together.

The *Leipzig* was fortunate enough to have had barges with tipples on both sides of her as she spent her day of fueling in San Francisco. When this operation was completed, she departed in the early hours of August 18 for her next announced destination, Honolulu, for additional coal. On her way out of port, thanks to a pilot who was apparently tipsy, she had a minor collision with an American sailing ship, with resultant damage to some topside areas of the cruiser.[15] It was certainly not an auspicious beginning for her new wartime service for the Kaiser.

Later that day, it appeared that she had not headed for Honolulu. She reportedly stopped the 3,300-ton American tanker *Catania*, 150 miles north of San Francisco, a thoroughly inexplicable act.[16] Captain Canty of the tanker reported that on this occasion the cruiser came bearing down on his ship which was not flying a national flag at the time. Through a flag hoist the *Leipzig* ordered the ship to identify herself and show her colors, which she promptly did, after which the cruiser sped away. There may be some confusion over dates of this incident; perhaps it took place during the north coast trip prior to the cruiser entering San Francisco. If that were the case, the German official reports indicated that the ships encountered by the cruiser on this trip "were not examined out of regard for American feelings," a statement that does not seem to rule out asking ships for identification. Moreover, the German official records contain no suggestion that such an incident could have taken place after the cruiser left San Francisco.

During the first part of August a confusing collection of cruiser sightings had been made by officers of well-known ships, sightings that had an authentic flavor, but are hard to accept. The Union Oil tanker *Lansing* reported encountering a German cruiser 70 miles south of Cape Flattery, Washington, on August 4; nationality was established when both the tanker and the cruiser hoisted national flags for the benefit of the other ship.[17] However, no German ship could have been there; the *Leipzig* was at Magdalena Bay and the *Nürnburg* would arrive at Ponape in the far Pacific on August 6. Since no reason existed for the British in *Newcastle* or the Canadians in *Rainbow* to hoist false colors, it is difficult to know what actually happened in this incident.

Similarly, the USS *Raleigh* sighted what her captain took to be the French cruiser *Montcalm* south of San Francisco; recognition was established through the ship's unusual configuration of two sets of stacks with a gap in between.[18] While other French cruisers also had the same arrangement of stacks, the cruisers of no other country displayed this profile. The *Montcalm* was reported to have been seen all over the Pacific Ocean early in the war, so there is no way of verifying this report.

The *Queen* of Pacific Coast Steamship in mid-August encountered a three-funnelled warship off Fort Bragg; this encounter could well have been with the *Leipzig* inasmuch as she had gone up the coast to Mendocino County before entering San Francisco.[19] Thus, these three encounters produced one utterly impossible identification, another possible but unlikely identification, and a third rather probable identification.

For many days following her departure from San Francisco the *Leipzig* was reported to have been detected along the Oregon, Washington, and British Columbia coasts. Inasmuch as British cruisers were known to be in British Columbia, there were rumors of cruisers stalking each other offshore. Residents of the central Oregon coast even reported hearing the gunfire of a major battle which they could detect being fought off the coast.

Clearly, the *Leipzig* had acquired a sinister reputation, even though she had not yet become a raider. In fact, the most violent thing she had done up to this point was shooting at and sinking her discarded ship's boats for target practice. Soon, however, she would become a genuine raider, and beyond that a ship of the line in a great sea battle that was to influence the course of the war.

CHAPTER THREE

COORDINATION, COMMUNICATION, AND COAL

The relative ease with which the Germans were able to supply their cruiser with needed coal in San Francisco during August of 1914 was due to the smooth coordination between several types of activity carried on by German nationals overseas in support of the country's foreign policy goals. This activity was conducted in a wide range of settings, including diplomatic, military, commercial, and individual. The most far-reaching coordination of the total logistics effort was carried out by the diplomatic establishment through which a German governmental presence existed all over the world, including the consulate in San Francisco.

The German diplomatic service was organized much along the lines of that of other countries, and included the standard listening-post functions that embassies and consulates normally exercise. With the rather sudden onset of the war, the German foreign office which had focused largely on neighboring countries in Europe was now called upon to expand its clandestine activities in many other parts of the world.[1]

In the United States, the German embassy was staffed by four executives: an ambassador, a commercial attaché, a military attaché, and a naval attaché. Inasmuch as no plans had existed for war with the United States, no organized secret service agency had been established within this country. The attachés served as the facilitators for whatever covert activities the German government felt were necessary. Considering that the United States was not regarded as a plum of an assignment for German diplomats, the key men who headed the German intelligence and espionage effort in the United States through the embassy were a remarkably effective quartet.

The ambassador to the United States was Count Johann Heinrich von Bernstorff, a suave and cosmopolitan career diplomat whose father, grandfather, and great-grandfather had each been an ambassador. Born in England, speaking flawless English and French, and possessing charm, manners, and patience, the count was the epitome both of the working diplomat and of the statesman. During his six years of tenure in this post prior to the outbreak of the war, he had been awarded five honorary degrees from American universities, including one from Princeton, the institution that Woodrow Wilson had once served as president. Von Bernstorff's primary responsibility as the senior German diplomat in the Western Hemisphere was to keep the United States out of the war. Quite possibly no other German had the credentials and talent to succeed in that mission as did this aristocratic but thoroughly likeable fourth-generation ambassador.

Shortly after the assassination of Archduke Ferdinand in Sarajevo in late June of 1914, Count von Bernsdorff had returned to Germany to consult with the German Foreign Office, and the several espionage and intelligence agencies of the General Staff and the Navy. He arrived back in the United States two days after the outbreak of war between England and Germany, with $150,000,000 in German treasury notes with which to finance German activities in the United States. Accompanying him on the trip to Berlin was Dr. Heinrich Albert, the commercial attaché.

Dr. Albert served as the Privy Councilor for the embassy in Washington, although he was headquartered in the Hamburg-American Line Building in New York to be near the financial markets of the United States. He was, in effect, the paymaster for the German war effort in America. It has been estimated that he eventually disbursed at least $30,000,000 for such clandestine activities as propaganda, sabotage, and various forms of espionage.[2] Like von Bernstorff, he was personable and well liked in the American circles in which he traveled; he was also highly regarded as an economist.

The third man in the German power structure in the United States was the military attaché, Major Franz von Papen. Because Berlin had not regarded Washington as a post which would result in a heavy workload for a military attaché, von Papen was also assigned to the German legation at Mexico City, where, thanks to the revolution, considerable military activity was taking place. A dashing young cavalry officer, von Papen projected a fine military appearance, but he was brash and outspoken and lacked the warmth and sincerity affected by von Bernstorff and Albert that endeared these men to the American officials with whom embassy personnel came in contact.

Rounding out the quartet of German officials was the naval attaché, Captain Karl Boy-Ed. The son of a German mother and a Turkish father, Boy-Ed had advanced rapidly in the

Kaiser's Navy, and had been given special executive training. Although he had a more rugged look than his fellow embassy staffers, he was a man of considerable polish and charm, and he exercised somewhat more discretion than the impulsive von Papen. Like Albert and von Papen, he was allowed to work out of an office in New York City.

From the embassy in Washington von Bernstorff exercised operational control over all the German activities that were carried out in the United States, with Dr. Albert supervising the finances, and von Papen and Boy-Ed handling the day-to-day details of such things as sabotage, gun running, obtaining false passports, and setting up cargo shipping conspiracies.

Each of the four men proved to have flaws of character or style which weakened his effectiveness. The urbane von Bernstorff tried to carry his facade of innocence too far; if any German agent were caught red-handed, the ambassador would always profess to know nothing of what had been going on, an attitude which in time weakened his credibility. In July, 1915, Dr. Albert committed a terrible faux pas for a foreign agent; he inadvertently left a briefcase full of important and revealing documents on an elevated train in New York while being followed by an American agent. The documents contained many details of undercover activity so embarrassing that von Bernstorff left on a ten-day vacation to avoid having to assert his ignorance of the incriminating events. Albert soon came to be known derisively as the "Minister without Portfolio."

The attachés, von Papen and Boy-Ed, each left too many paper trails in carrying out their dirty work. A German agent named Archibald was arrested upon his arrival in England from the United States; his luggage contained, among other things, canceled checks and payments made by the attachés to saboteurs, as well as records of the various acts committed by these agents. There were also records of frequent dealings of the attachés with former Mexican president Vittoriano Huerta, and details of other transactions in Mexico which were designed to embarrass the United States. Newspapers printed so many of the disclosures from the captured briefcase and luggage that President Wilson felt compelled to ask for the recall of the two attachés as *persona non grata*. The Germans complied; Boy-Ed and von Papen had to give up the good life of New York and return to Germany.

Wolf von Igel, von Papen's successor did not fare much better. In 1916 four federal agents entered von Igel's office while his safe was standing open. Demonstrating a new-found aggressiveness against the Germans, these agents physically restrained the attaché while they took from the safe a number of documents which showed additional violations of American neutrality by German agents. Although von Igel had screamed "This means war!" during this incident, German leaders, albeit disturbed by the breach of diplomatic immunity, were obviously not about to go to war with the very nation they had been trying to keep out of the war.

In carrying out maritime or naval activities in the United States in support of their cause, the Germans found it necessary to establish a communication and supply system that made use of the embassy and consulates but was essentially operated from naval headquarters in Berlin. For this purpose the *Etappe* system was devised and put into place well before the war began. Originally a French word for stage or base, the Germans borrowed the term to use in a military sense to denote lines of communication or a network. Known collectively as *Etappen*, this system made use of supply contacts around the world through which the coal, water, and other supply needs of warships and raiders could be met.

The oceans were divided into areas served by operational control centers, generally an embassy or consulate in a major port, under the command of a naval officer. Although at the outset of the war many of the world's merchant ships did not have radios, vessels of all the major German shipping firms were equipped with receiving and transmitting sets, and the masters had been provided sealed orders to be opened in time of war or national emergency. The sealed orders included the assignment of each ship to a regional *Etappe*.

In the Pacific, the regional centers included the German naval base at Tsingtao in China, and offices in Tokyo, Manila, Batavia, Valparaiso, Callao, and San Francisco, plus Dar-Es-Salaam in German Southwest Africa which served the Indian Ocean.[3] Each of these offices had cells in various ports within its region where German diplomatic personnel and businessmen could provide for the needs of ships that were directed there. For example, the San Francisco *Etappe* had jurisdiction over the port of Guaymas and over the *Mazatlan,*

Marie, and other German vessels along the Mexican coast. The coaling of the *Leipzig* at Guaymas, described in later chapters, illustrated the interaction between the major components of the German supply system. The delivery of the fuel was ordered by the naval authorities, coordinated and managed by diplomatic personnel through the consulates in San Francisco and Guaymas, provided with an innocent-sounding cover as well as with cooperative shipmasters by the business community in both ports, and supported enthusiastically by the efforts of private citizens of German nationality.

In the non-military components of this supply system, such as the consular staffs and the business community, frequently the important leaders also held reserve commissions in the German armed forces. In San Francisco at the start of the war the newspapers made a big fuss over the loyal Germans at the consulate and throughout the Bay Area who were now preparing for immediate departure on eastbound trains in order to embark as soon as possible for their native land to serve their country.[4] In reality, however, most people in the German community in and around San Francisco stayed where they were, providing the *Etappe* a reservoir of talent and connections from which to draw.

The consulate in the Bay Area was staffed with a group of professional foreign service officers who must have been fairly typical of those sent to important posts. The consul general, rotund and middle-aged Franz Bopp, was on leave in Germany when the war began, and did not return to his post until March of 1915. Acting in his absence was the vice consul, Baron Eckhardt H. von Schack, a young man who would later be criticized in both American and German circles as being a bit out of his league because of his immaturity. Assisting him was the elderly Henry Kaufmann, the councilor or financial agent of the consulate, and a young reserve officer in the German Army, Wilhelm von Brincken, who was a military attaché of sorts.

In San Francisco and throughout the world, the success of the *Etappen* depended in large measure on good radio communication. Reliable long-range radio transmission was not yet a reality in 1914, so it was necessary for Germany to establish a series of overseas radio stations that could relay messages across the broad distances of the Pacific. For the first few months of the war these stations were helpful to the

Above, the cruiser USS *California* was instrumental in relaying to German and British men-of-war the news that World War One had begun, and in relieving them of their refugee passengers who were fleeing the revolution in Mexico. Below, the German cruiser *Leipzig* was allowed to coal during a 24-hour visit to San Francisco shortly after the war began. The surplus coal acquired during this visit would later lead to a test of American neutrality laws.

Above, the *Leipzig* completed her coaling at the Mexican port of Guaymas and set out to join the German cruiser squadron. The logistic needs of this ship set in motion the San Francisco conspiracies of 1914-15. Below, the German-owned freighter *Mazatlan* played the initial role in carrying out the coal shipments which had first been approved by American authorities who later treated them as serious neutrality violations.

hundreds of German merchant ships which were still at sea, including a number of colliers, but soon the British were able to locate and silence most of these stations. However, American authorities were never quite satisfied that all of them had been discovered, particularly in Mexico.

German planners were realistic enough to know that any bases and radio stations in their possession at the outset of the war would not last long. For this reason, the design of the *Etappen* as well as the concept of the surface raider required the existence of a large number of colliers which could supply cruisers or merchant raiders at pre-arranged rendezvous points at isolated islands or anchorages. As a fuel, coal had one distinct advantage; it could be stored in simple piles that could be created anywhere. Furthermore, it required no technology to move; a few men with shovels could suffice in a pinch, although the work was physically strenuous. Any freighter was a potential collier, and every harbor was a potential coaling station. Offsetting the advantages of simplicity of handling was the amount of bulk space that coal consumed. German warships literally could not cross the Pacific non-stop because they could not carry enough coal in their bunkers to make the trip, even at reduced speed.

Oil on the other hand was not easy to store and move; it required tanks, pipelines, and pumps, plus specialized ships for transportation. But it stowed well, and in most ships a thirty-day supply could be accommodated without constructing oversize tanks. Consequently, it is interesting to speculate about the raiders of World War One if they had been oil burners instead of coal-fired ships.

Nevertheless, coal was the reality. When the war began, a number of colliers were available all over the world, and the German East Asia squadron to which the *Leipzig* and *Nürnberg* belonged, while it had to operate frugally, was never really short of fuel to the point of having to restrict operations. However, had these ships been called upon to survive another six months at sea the story would have been quite different. The colliers which before the start of the war had readily acquired coal at any place in the world would now have to find their way to neutral nations in whose ports they could refill their cargo holds for the next round of coaling.

The dominant British and Japanese presence in the Far East ruled out ports in the western Pacific as a source of coal. This left the neutral countries of the west coast of the Americas — Chile, Peru, Ecuador, the Central American republics, Mexico, and the United States — as the likely source for any resupply of the vital fuel. In most of these areas, Germany enjoyed warm relations with the national government which would have to approve the loading of coal destined for a belligerent man-of-war, an action that represented one of the grey areas of international law. If the United States could not be regarded as one of those friendly governments, the Germans could always capitalize upon the naiveté and gullibility that Americans were showing as neutrals to get around any problems that might prevent colliers taking fuel to cruisers. However, that is getting ahead of our story.

The question of whether the German colliers could have found their replenishment coal in these neutral countries became in time an academic one, however, when the need for the coal ceased with the passing of the cruiser fleet. But that, too, is getting ahead of our story.

CHAPTER FOUR

THE *LEIPZIG* GOES TO WAR

After leaving San Francisco, instead of journeying on her rumored foray to the north or proceeding to Hawaii on her announced passage, the *Leipzig* actually had changed course and headed for Mexican waters at an economical seven-knot speed. She was headed for an anticipated rendezvous along the coast of Baja with another freighter carrying coal, the *Mazatlan*. This small steamer had been owned by German interests, but now had recently been re-registered from the German to the Mexican flag.[1]

American authorities had first been reluctant to let this merchant ship leave San Francisco on her scheduled voyage to Guaymas in the State of Sonora in the Gulf of California. The ship was well known in San Francisco, and had presented no problems in the past. However, an innocent accident of a small fire in the bagged coal on deck had called attention of the local port authorities to the ship's cargo. The subsequent reluctance of the authorities to clear the vessel reflected the fact that Captain R. J. Paulsen and his officers were suspected of intending to deliver the coal to the German cruiser at sea, since the cargo of sacked coal had originally been acquired as a part of the abortive plan to fuel the *Leipzig* at sea with tug and lighter. Furthermore, since the coal had been bought and paid for by the Germans as a part of the purchase arranged by the consulate, it seemed only natural, and perhaps only fair as well, that the coal would eventually reach the cruiser.[2]

While the *Mazatlan* was awaiting clearance for her scheduled trip to Guaymas with a cargo which now included the coal as well as general merchandise, the torpedo boat destroyer, USS *Preble*, was given the assignment of watching her, and of detaining the ship if she tried to leave San Francisco without receiving clearance.[3] No armed intervention was necessary, however, during the time the freighter remained in port.

The official consignor of the coal had become F. G. Braue who claimed that he had been commissioned to sell the coal for the consulate, with the consignee being the Mexican firm of W. Iberri in Guaymas. The collector of customs in the Bay Area, John O. Davis, who was responsible for granting clearances for ships to sail, telegraphed Collector of Customs Halstead in Washington and his boss, Secretary of the Treasury William G.

McAdoo, for guidance in responding to the request for clearance for the *Mazatlan.* McAdoo, in turn, referred the question to Robert Lansing, Counselor of the State Department, who asked the Joint State and Navy Neutrality Board for an opinion. Inasmuch as the war had been underway for only two weeks, it is surprising that the answer came back rather quickly. The decision, based on the Hague Convention of 1907, specified that the ship would be allowed to sail, if it were understood by all parties that the coal on board would not be delivered directly to a German war vessel which had already received coal in a United States port within the past three months—which, of course, the *Leipzig* had. Another condition was put on the permission to sail, that if a German vessel were to receive the coal, that vessel could not coal again in the United States for three months.[4]

These conditions did not bother the Germans, since they knew the *Leipzig* was leaving the west coast of North America. As a show of good faith, however, the German consul in San Francisco, Baron E. H. von Schack, and the owner of the *Mazatlan,* Fredrich Jebsen, agreed to post a substantial cash bond. This bond was valued at $11,400, more than the value of the 7,143 sacks of coal on board; it assured the authorities that the *Mazatlan* would deliver the cargo to its consignee at that port.[5]

The name of the shipowner, Fred Jebsen, would soon begin to show up repeatedly in connection with German activities, as the *Etappe* in San Francisco drew further upon his expertise in shipping. The scion of a prominent Hamburg shipping family and a reserve officer in the German Navy, Jebsen was a dedicated and dangerous man, although described as personable and well-liked in west coast shipping circles. Within a short period of time he would become the most resourceful of the German conspirators, only to drop from sight less than ten months after the start of the war, to resurface within weeks in Germany as an officer of the submarine, U-36.

Upon being cleared to depart from the Golden Gate, the *Mazatlan* steamed south toward her Mexican destination. Although the British argued later that she had not been cleared for such a stop,[6] she put into San Pedro where her owner, Fred Jebsen and two officers from the *Leipzig* boarded her, Oberleutnant a. D. zur Helle and the supply officer, Dr. Simon

Reimer. The radio officer of the freighter, G. D. Smith, would later report that a German radio officer, Gustave Traub, also came aboard at San Pedro.[7] Two women, an Anna Speddin and a Grace Crim who were sisters, each divorced, also came on board at this port as passengers.

After a stop at Ensenada, the ship reached Whale Bay, another of the secluded anchorages halfway down the Baja peninsula, on August 27. As the American authorities had feared, the *Mazatlan* met the German cruiser there. As soon as the two vessels anchored close to each other, Jebsen and zur Helle rowed over to the cruiser and spent several hours aboard her. Apparently, the meeting was a cordial affair. The freeighter's captain, R. J. Paulsen observed later with a disapproving tone that wicker-enclosed champagne bottles were floating in great profusion around the *Leipzig*.

Paulsen also commented on the fact that Jebsen had gotten chummy with one of his female passengers during the voyage.[8] Later, Jebsen confided to a friend that he was concerned that he might get picked up for violating the Mann Act as a result of having the women aboard.[9] It was ironic that the Mann Act could trip up miscreants who could not be caught any other way. The German captain of the interned *Prinz Eitel Friedrich* was arrested and convicted for such a violation on the east coast of the United States.[10]

In spite of the cordiality of the meeting at Whale Bay, the *Mazatlan*, in keeping with the terms of her bond, provided no coal to the cruiser during this visit. Captain Haun of the *Leipzig* had hoped that with the coal from the *Mazatlan* aboard he could then head south, coaling again at Socorro Island from the *Marie*, a freighter owned by the Jebsen family which had recently arrived from the Orient and was then ready to load additional coal at Guaymas. Nevertheless, Haun respected the position of Captain Paulsen of the *Mazatlan* and that of Jebsen in whose name the bond had been granted. The two captains then agreed that the next coaling of the cruiser would have to take place in the Gulf of California after the cargo of coal had been delivered at Guaymas.

Coal had become the Achilles heel of the *Leipzig*. The cruiser had a capacity in her bunker spaces of 822 tons, but she consumed the bulky fuel at the rate of 196 tons per day when steaming at 20 knots, 82 tons per day at 15 knots, or 40 tons per day at 10 knots.[11] With these consumption rates, after four days of steaming at high speed she would be desperately short of coal again. Consequently, every move that the ship made was governed closely by the availability of coal.

Although the *Mazatlan*, after a stop at San Jose del Cabo, was able to enter the Gulf unmolested, the cruiser was forced to wait several more days concealed at Whale Bay before running the risk of detection in getting underway again. Keeping a close lookout for the British cruiser *Newcastle* which was known to be looking for her, the *Leipzig* entered the Gulf on the night of August 31. En route, an American steamer exchanged blinker signals with her, asking the usual question, "What ship?" Knowing that a cruiser is difficult to disguise, even at night, Captain Haun had his signalman identify his ship as the Japanese *Idzumo*, a reply that satisfied the curious American officer.[12] There was an irony in Haun's tactic on this occasion. The Japanese cruiser had left San Diego at about the same time the *Leipzig* had left San Francisco, but Japan had not yet entered the war at that time. Following Japan's declaration of war on August 23, 1914, the *Idzumo* had tried to establish contact with the German cruiser, but had apparently gone north in looking for her.

Once inside the Gulf, the *Leipzig* proceeded to Concepcion Bay, another excellent isolated anchorage near Mulege on the peninsula coastline. There she waited in a small cove within the bay for two and a half sweltering days in the expectation that the *Mazatlan* would have reached Guaymas by this time and discharged her coal in compliance with her bond. Upon completion of that delivery, a smaller vessel was to bring some of the coal across the Gulf to the *Leipzig*.

Both Germany and Great Britain maintained resident part-time consuls in Guaymas. These officials, Otto Rademacher and William Fearon, respectively, were prominent businessmen in the city, each of whom had influence with the local authorities. These two men now began to play a cat and mouse game with the bagged coal which the *Mazatlan* was ready to discharge. Fearon, the British consul, suspicious of what might be going on, was able to get the coal discharged into lighters, rather than into the hold of the *Lenora*, a 128-foot schooner owned by Fred Jebsen which the Germans had planned to use in delivering the coal to the cruiser at

Concepcion Bay, 90 miles to the southwest. Rademacher, the German consul, countered by acquiring additional bulk coal from the ample supply of the Sonora Railroad, two thousand tons of it in railroad cars which could be taken directly out onto the pier. However, it would now take many hours to load the coal into the *Lenora*, and she would have been able to take only about 400 tons of it; consequently, a decision had to be made to resolve the logistics problem more satisfactorily.[13]

The Germans briefly considered bringing to Guaymas one of the dozen German square-rigged sailing ships which had elected to ride out the war at Santa Rosalia, a copper mining port across the Gulf; this large ship could then load a full cargo of coal for the cruiser. This idea, however, was soon set aside as being too time-consuming, although the ship *Lasbek* did sail across to Guaymas later that fall as part of an ill-conceived scheme to utilize her in the future as a collier for the *Leipzig*.[14]

The decision was then made by Rademacher and the cruiser's officers who had arrived aboard the *Mazatlan* that the *Leipzig* would have to come to Guaymas for the coal. Getting the word to the cruiser now became the next challenge for the Germans. To avoid tipping off anyone to the presence of the warship, they decided not to use radio in contacting her. Oberleutnant zur Helle, a retired officer who appears to have been a merchant captain with a reserve commission, was then dispatched in an auxiliary schooner to sail across the Gulf in search of the ship.

An officer in a rag-tag German uniform appeared briefly and mysteriously in the middle of the night at the laid-up German sailing fleet in Santa Rosalia at about this same time, asking if there were any charts of the northern Gulf which he could take with him. This man may have been zur Helle who was looking for the cruiser. In any case, the ship was soon found. When she was located at her hidden anchorage in Concepcion Bay the evening of September 6, the *Leipzig* had only one hundred and fifty tons of coal remaining in her bunkers. Captain Haun quickly agreed with zur Helle that he had no other option; the cruiser weighed anchor and departed for the port on the mainland. By noon of the following day she was tied up at the railroad pier at Empalme in a bay adjacent to Guaymas Bay, much to the surprise of the British consul and the officers of the USS *Albany* which was in port looking after American refugees. As a neutral, of course, there was nothing that the American cruiser could do about the presence of the German warship, but consul Fearon was soon in touch with the British embassy in Mexico City.[15]

During the next twenty four hours the German warship frantically took on board a full load of bulk coal, and piled an additional 125 tons of the bagged coal from the *Mazatlan* on her decks, giving her a total of roughly 950 tons on board—still only enough for five days of high-speed steaming. The loading was supervised by Jebsen, zur Helle, and Traub. When this task was completed the cruiser unceremoniously stood out to sea, but not before Captain Haun had been assured by the German agents ashore that another collier, the 7,000-ton *Amasis* of the Kosmos Line was en route from Callao, Peru, to the Galapagos Islands with 3,000 additional tons of coal for him. Coaling there was necessary because this first leg of the voyage south was about 2,100 miles in length, which at 15 knots could consume half the coal on board.

The balance of the coal on the pier was loaded aboard the SS *Marie.* This ship had helped to evacuate Americans from Mexico to California earlier in 1914; now as one of the ships of the German Navy's *Etappen* she left Guaymas four hours after the *Leipzig* to serve as a collier and a water supply ship for at least the next several weeks. However, Captain J. Davidson of this ship proved to be rather uncooperative, so the captain of the cruiser was forced to threaten the merchant captain with discharge as well as to place a supercargo aboard, in the person of the omnipresent Lieutenant zur Helle, in order to obtain compliance from his collier's captain.[16]

Moving south at an economical speed toward the open ocean 300 miles away, the crew of the *Leipzig* hosed down her decks to get rid of the penetrating coal dust as the cruiser prepared to leave Mexico forever. Finally on September 10, 1914, she cleared the Gulf for the open sea, unaware that a British cruiser, the *Newcastle*, had been reported at Mazatlan on the previous day and would be reported at Magdalena Bay on the 15th—creating a trackline that would come uncomfortably close to the German cruiser.[17] Unperturbed, she continued on south to join her old unit, the German East Asian squadron coming across the Pacific after detaching the cruiser *Emden* on her soon-to-be-famous raiding voyage into the Indian Ocean.

Once the *Leipzig* was gone, it looked as if the German businessmen of Guaymas through Rademacher had been able to out-maneuver their British counterparts. However, these apparent winners ultimately paid the price for their complicity. The British were able to get the German firm to which the coal had been consigned, W. Iberri and Sons, placed on a blacklist which carried over into an American blacklist after the United States entered the war. Eventually, the firm was forced out of business.[18]

Although most of the *Leipzig*'s furtive scurrying about had centered around her efforts to get an adequate supply of coal to supply her fuel-gobbling engineering plant as well as in dodging the allied cruisers that were looking for her, the ship finally engaged in one successful surface action off the Mexican coast, which made her a bona fide German raider in North American waters. En route to freedom in September, 1914, only one day out of the Gulf and five weeks after the start of the war, she captured and sank with gunfire the 6,500-ton British tanker *Elsinore* about 80 miles off the coast.[19] This year-old ship had been en route in ballast from Corinto, Nicaragua, to Port San Luis, an oil loading port on the central California coast. In keeping with the practice of her squadron-mate early in the war, the soon-to-be-famous and romantic raider *Emden*, the *Leipzig* subsequently utilized her collier *Marie* to land Captain John Roberts and the crew of the tanker safely in the Galapagos Islands, from which point within a few days they were able to obtain passage to the South American mainland.

There is an interesting footnote to the sinking of this ship. The *Elsinore* was reportedly listed as one of the vessels controlled by the San Francisco office of the German *Etappen*. One authority on World War I German naval activity indicates that the Germans operated her for a few days with Oberleutnant zur Helle in command,[20] but the official record of the cruiser fleet includes no such service. Inasmuch as German cruisers were coal burners and no submarines were known to be operating in the Pacific, it is not clear why the Germans would have needed an empty tanker at this time and place. By the same token, however, it is not easy to identify an alternative trade in which the British ship would be operating on the west coast of Mexico in 1914 so soon after the opening of the

Panama Canal in August. Thus, the *Elsinore* and any ties she might have had to the Germans remain a mystery.

After having sunk a British freighter whose crew was taken to Callao aboard the *Marie*, the *Leipzig* eventually reached Easter Island in the South Pacific; there on October 14 she joined four other German cruisers, including the *Nürnberg* which had been at Guaymas earlier that year, and their colliers. Cruising south, on November 1, 1914, these ships met a British squadron of warships off the coast of Chile. In this engagement, generally known as the Battle of Coronel, the Germans outmaneuvered the British cruisers which had been sent to intercept them, and sank several of their adversaries.[21] At least two of the German ships taking part in this action were fueled in part by coal that had come from Guaymas and/or San Francisco.

After the battle, the cruisers spent a week, along with their colliers, at Mas Afuera, the island off the coast of Chile which Daniel Defoe had described in *Robinson Crusoe*. Thanks to the *Sacramento*, the former Hamburg-American Line freighter *Alexandria* which had recently been reflagged in San Francisco as an American ship, there was plenty of additional coal and supplies for the cruisers and the colliers they would take with them as they went south.

A few weeks later the British had their revenge at the Falkland Islands, when the *Leipzig*, together with all but one of the other German cruisers, was finally sunk by the Royal Navy. Accounts of the battle describe how Captain Haun calmly smoked a cigar as his ship was sinking, and refused to strike his colors even though his ship had exhausted her ammunition and torpedoes. Some British naval historians theorize that the Germans lost the element of surprise in the Falklands by arriving late, the result of the capture by the *Leipzig* of the iron four-masted bark *Drummuir* east of Cape Horn. This ship, home-ported in British Columbia but managed by the firm owned by Jim Rolph, the mayor of San Francisco, was taken to an island anchorage where her cargo of coal was used to fill the bunkers of the German cruisers in Admiral von Spee's squadron. The advantage of being amply supplied with coal was subsequently canceled out by the late arrival of the German ships at the Falklands, where the British beat them decisively, with only the *Dresden* getting away. Thus, the

Leipzig had not only lived by her ability to acquire coal, but she brought on her own premature demise, as well as that of several other German warships, by being too successful—or perhaps too greedy—in using that ability.

The immediate fate of the *Marie* is not clear. Her captain had been overly talkative in Callao, and the Germans were relieved to be able to cut their ties with the unreliable ship.[22] Had she not belonged to Jebsen, she might easily have been sunk. She was apparently given her freedom along the Peruvian coast before the *Leipzig* went to Easter Island for the gathering of the German cruiser squadron there; thus she was not at the Battle of Coronel nor at the week-long replenishment rendezvous at Mas Afuera Island after that battle. She may have been interned in Peru. In contrast, shipping columns continued to mention the *Mazatlan* as she traded on the Mexican coast, risking encounters with British men-of-war.

However, the *Mazatlan* had a checkered future ahead of her. One unverified report indicates that she was wrecked near Topolobampo in 1915 with her crew rescued by an American cruiser.[23] Other reliable reports make clear that she was detained for several months in Ensenada, first by Villista forces and then by Governor Cantu, during which time she was occupied by soldiers and beached to become a fortress guarding the port.[24] Still others indicate that, after being re-flagged American as the *Edna*, she was seized by the British as a prize in 1916 while carrying a cargo of nitrate to the West Indies under charter to the Grace Line, taken to the Falkland Islands, and not returned to her owners until 1921.[25] Reportedly, the tangled ownership of the ship was not straightened out for another twenty years.[26]

When it had become evident how the *Leipzig* had obtained her coal in Guaymas, as well as how a German collier had loaded from the same supply, the British expressed their concern to the United States, asking why the *Mazatlan*, for which the bond had now been satisfied, was allowed to sail from San Francisco with the knowledge that she was supplying the *Leipzig*. The British were also concerned that the San Francisco firm that they identified as J. J. Moore & Company, which had sent the coal on the *Mazatlan*, had recently followed up by chartering the British freighter *Banksdale* and loading her with 6,000 tons of coal for delivery in Guaymas.[27] The

American diplomatic reply pointed out that there was nothing contrary to international law in allowing the coal to be shipped to Guaymas; what happened to the coal once at its destination was not the concern of the United States.[28] This posture would soon prove to be fraught with trouble for the American authorities.

The British were not satisfied with this reply, and they pressed the matter further through their ambassador in the United States, Cecil Spring Rice. One development which bothered the British was the acknowledgment by the former radio operator of the *Mazatlan*, G. D. Smith, that the ship had not only transferred coal to the *Marie* for the *Leipzig*, but that he had been asked to communicate directly by radio with the German cruiser. Fred Jebsen had threatened him if he did not do so, so the young British-born wireless operator had put the set out of commission rather than comply with Jebsen's demands. Smith subsequently left the *Mazatlan* and went home to England on a British ship.[29]

The French added their voice to the criticisms that the British were raising with respect to coal shipments. The French ambassador, Jean Jules Jusserand, pointed out to the Secretary of State that the American ship *Rio Pasig* in August had loaded 4,000 tons of coal at Manila, bound for Guam, but upon arrival there had not delivered the cargo and instead had headed off in a direction suggesting that she was looking for the German cruiser fleet. Secretary Bryan replied in effect that the situation was moot, in that while the ship did depart from her scheduled route she was subsequently seized by a British destroyer off Zamboango in the Philippines, and was interned in British North Borneo.[30] Later, when the official history of German cruiser warfare was written, it became clear that the Germans indeed had expected the *Rio Pasig* to deliver coal to their assembly point in the northern Marianas.[31]

Curiously, this incident does not seem to have generated much interest within the State Department. Presumably, the capture of an American merchant ship at sea in the Philippines with a cargo that was contraband only in the conditional sense, and the subsequent internment of that ship in a distant colony of the belligerent nation would call for an exchange of notes, but none seems to have been forthcoming. The question was soon academic, however, in that the British put the ship into service under their flag, after which she was lost on a voyage between Puget Sound and Vladivostock in 1916. Perhaps the official indifference by the federal government to this confiscation reflected the fact that the ship, although flying the American flag, was owned by a Philippine concern and not by a firm domiciled in the United States.

All that the State Department could muster to counter the criticisms of American naiveté about these coal shipments was to point out that the British may have been overreacting in the matter of coal. A British ship, *Lowther Range*, under charter to the San Francisco firm of Moore & Company to carry coal from Newcastle, Australia, to Guaymas, Mexico, for the American-owned Southern Pacific Railroad, certainly a legitimate user of the fuel, had been stopped by the cruiser *Newcastle* off Guaymas, and, after helping herself to the coal she needed, the cruiser sent the merchant ship with a prize crew north to British Columbia. "Clean up your own act," was the inference in the State Department message to the British,[32] but it was obvious that American officials were chagrined at being duped by the Germans and scolded for it by the British.

After the departure of the *Leipzig*, rumors of other German naval vessels in North American waters continued to surface. Two allied cruisers, the British *Newcastle* and the Japanese *Idzumo*, coaled from the British ship *Protesilaus* near Guadalupe Island off the Mexican coast in mid-November, 1914, still expecting the German fleet to come north.[33] Early in 1915 a newspaper reporter at Turtle Bay on the Pacific Coast of Baja California was told by officers of a Japanese cruiser that there were German warships nearby.[34] At the same time the captain of a Mexican patrol vessel was quoted by newsmen as saying that he had recently seen a mysterious two-stacked cruiser with no identifying national flag in the anchorage at Magdalena Bay, several hundred miles south of Turtle Bay.[35]

In 1916, off the central Mexican coast, the Canadian naval vessel *Rainbow* took as a prize the schooner *Lenora*, which had been a pawn in the plan to fuel the *Leipzig* in the Gulf of California two years earlier. Still under the operational control of the Germans in Guaymas when seized, the vessel was towed to Canada and interned as a Mexican-flag merchant vessel which had violated her neutrality.[36]

However, no confirmed sightings of German naval vessels occurred on the west coast of North America throughout the rest of the war. Nevertheless, there would soon be other merchant ships along the Pacific coast of North and South America with curious links to Germany and the German Navy, ships that would create trouble in their own way.

CHAPTER FIVE

ENTER THE *SACRAMENTO*

The acting German consul in San Francisco, 33-year old Eckhardt H. von Schack, was pleased that everything had gone so well with the coaling of the *Leipzig* from the supply that was sent to Guaymas aboard the *Mazatlan*, the balance of which subsequently reached the cruiser at the Galapagos Islands on the *Marie*. Now it was time to think in terms of meeting the greater needs of the German cruiser squadron, coming across the Pacific from China by a circuitous route.

Baron von Schack, the personification of the monocle-wearing Prussian diplomat, was acting consul in the absence of Franz Bopp who had been caught by the start of the war while vacationing in Europe. Von Schack was aware that a large freighter of the Hamburg-American Line, the SS *Alexandria*, had arrived in port on August 7, 1914, after coming up the coast within the safety of the three mile limit, a measure necessitated by the declaration of war on August 4. She had arrived ten days ahead of the *Leipzig* which she had encountered off the tip of Baja California.[1] Built in England in 1900, this freighter was 451 feet long, 52 feet in beam, and 28 feet deep, measuring out at 5,692 gross tons. Her ample hull was well-powered with a triple expansion reciprocating steam engine that produced 3,700 indicated horsepower. In recent years this ship had been running between Hamburg and the west coast of South America; on the trip which was just concluding she had been under charter to the Kosmos Line, another German firm.[2]

The circumstances of this ship's arrival at San Francisco immediately after the start of the war were subject to some variation in reporting. The local shipping journal, *The Guide*, reported that she arrived in ballast from Callao with 50 passengers aboard,[3] but the authoritative *Maritime Register* of New York indicated that she had touched only in Costa Rica and Guatemala after leaving Chile.[4] The official German version, contained in volume one of *Der Krieg zur See 1914-1918*, said that she had a cargo of ore on board destined for British Columbia.[5] Neither of these latter sources said anything about passengers.

Partial confirmation of the ship's northern destination was contained in shipping notices in Seattle papers that she was expected there on August 17.[6]   However, references to her cargo in shipping columns in San Francisco make no mention of an ore cargo but suggest instead that she had on board about 2,000 tons of merchandise.[7] Upon the *Alexandria's* arrival, it was apparent that she did have at least one passenger aboard, but this person turned out to be Dr. Simon Reimer who had boarded the ship from the *Leipzig*.[8]

Her radio instructions from the *Leipzig* had directed that she should discharge her cargo as quickly as possible and make herself ready for serving the needs of the cruiser,[9] but those instructions were issued while war was imminent but not yet officially declared. Now it was obvious that she was coming into a neutral port as a merchant ship of a belligerent country. As it turned out, her arrival at the Golden Gate had been only two hours ahead of that of the Canadian cruiser *Rainbow*, one of the three allied cruisers known to be on the west coast; consequently, there was less risk for the freighter in entering port than in countering her earlier orders and trying to remain at sea.[10]

Regardless of where she had been, where she was going, and what she had on board, the *Alexandria* was a German ship; this meant that unless she wanted to run the risk of leaving the harbor, she was for all practical purposes bottled up in a United States port for the duration of the war. For more than a month she would lie at anchor in Richardson Bay, across the Golden Gate from San Francisco, while the staff of the German consulate was putting together its next move.

Even before the *Leipzig* was clear of North American waters, officials of the San Francisco *Etappe* were making plans for utilizing the bulk capacity of the *Alexandria* in support of the German war effort. Eventually they came up with a scheme that was as simple as it was audacious: change the ship's registration to that of the United States, and use her to supply the cruisers which were moving toward the west coast of South America. Aware of how gullible the local port authorities had been during the *Mazatlan* affair, the Germans decided that it would be relatively easy to create a dummy American corporation, buy the ship under the provisions of a new federal law which had been adopted in mid-August, and sail her with a cargo of American coal under the American flag to the coast of South America to replenish the German fleet.

The company that was hurriedly established for the purpose was a California corporation bearing the name Northern and Southern Steamship Company. Originally, it was not clear exactly who the owners of record of the corporation were, but later it became evident that several prominent American shipping men were the actual stockholders. These men were: Robert H. Swayne and John G. Hoyt of the steamship company Swayne & Hoyt which put in $122,500 of the total capital; Philip R. Thayer, a local businessman who dabbled in shipping through the ownership of a four-masted barque, who contributed $5,000; and two others, otherwise unidentified, E. B. de Golia whose investment was $5,000, and P. S. Teller who invested $2,500.[11] The capital stock of the firm was then placed in an escrow arrangement between the company and Louis T. Hengstler, an admiralty attorney who was formerly on the faculty of the University of California and who now represented the German consulate.[12]

This agreement provided that the company could not see or have possession of its own stock except in the presence of Hengstler who concurrently made a declaration of trust in favor of the German government. Furthermore, after the end of hostilities between Germany and England, Hengstler could make whatever use of the shares that he saw fit, and the corporation would have no claim on its own stock. Each of the three Americans who engineered this transaction received $7,500 from the Germans for his efforts in setting up the corporate shell. These men were all respected members of the shipping community in San Francisco: Robert H. Swayne of the steamship company Swayne & Hoyt, and Joseph L. Bley and C. D. Bunker, each of C. D. Bunker & Company, a customs house brokerage firm.[13]

The acquisition of the ship was negotiated for the buyers by Philip R. Thayer. Representing the sellers was Harold Ebey, who was the San Francisco agent for the Kosmos Line and Hamburg American.[14] On September 21, Northern and Southern Steamship Company completed the purchase of the ship and filed the bill of sale with the Collector of Customs in San Francisco.[15] On the following day the new company applied to the United States Department of Commerce for registration of the ship under the name, *Sacramento*. At about this same time the ship was shifted from the anchorage to San Francisco for loading.

By October 1 she had completed loading a cargo of coal which has been described in various sources as 4,000 to 7,000 tons, along with about another 1,000 tons of general cargo. The coal was obtained from Rolph Coal and Navigation Company, owned by the then-mayor of San Francisco and later governor of California, "Sunny Jim" Rolph. The price was $9 per ton, with the total price of $59,211 suggesting that 6,587 tons were purchased. The actual contract specified that the $9 price applied to the first five thousand tons, after which all additional coal would cost $12 a ton. On this basis, 6,184 tons would have been acquired for the $59,211 total price.[16]

The buyer was the C. D. Bunker Company which became the consignor of the coal. Joseph L. Bley, co-owner of the Bunker Company, appeared at a hearing before the Collector of Customs in San Francisco and claimed that the cargo was purchased by the Banco Mexicano de Commercio E Industria. However, John W. Preston, the district attorney, later indicated that the Mexican bank had simply laundered the money, which actually represented German funds on deposit with the Crocker and Wells Fargo banks. The purchase price of the ship, the $64,000 in freight paid for the transportation of the cargo, and the $43,000 of provisions had all been handled in similar fashion. In each case, German money came back to German hands.[17]

On October 3, even before the change of flag had been approved, the owners of the ship applied for immediate clearance of the vessel from San Francisco with her cargo of coal and merchandise to Valparaiso. This haste on the part of the Germans made the local authorities a bit suspicious, so on that same day the Navy placed an armed guard from the USS New Orleans on board to insure that the ship was not moved and that her radio was not used. Although the local German officials made only token protests of this action, the German Ambassador in Washington lodged a formal protest concerning the guard on board, pointing out that the ship was still German and that neither the change of registration nor the clearance had been granted.[18]

During the next few days, many messages flew back and forth between Washington and San Francisco over the legal issues involved in the transfer. Practical considerations were also discussed, such as the argument of the British consul in San Francisco to the effect that since American coal was cheaper in Valparaiso than in San Francisco—only about £1.6 or roughly $8.00—it was likely that this coal was intended for German warships, not for the Valparaiso Power and Light Company to which it was consigned.[19]

In the meantime, the local authorities in San Francisco, apparently now aware that they had been tricked in the case of the *Mazatlan*, were uneasy about what was going on aboard the *Alexandria*. One suspicious factor was the sale price of the vessel, $135,000, well below the going price for a large well-powered freighter in wartime. Another was the obvious strong link between the people of the Kosmos Line and the new company which had been formed to operate the ship. Still another was the economics of the shipment, in which coal costing $9 a ton would be shipped at a cost of almost $10 a ton to Chile where good American coal was available for $8 a ton. The U. S. Shipping Commissioner for the port of San Francisco at that time, Walter Macarthur, recalled that, like the *Mazatlan* case, "guarantees were demanded and given; and bonds were put up to guarantee against misuse of the American flag."[20]

The official position being developed in Washington was that the transfer of the ship to American registry must be a bona fide act that changed the nature of the ownership and loyalty of the vessel out of foreign into American hands. In general, the American view incorporated the intent of the Declaration of London of 1909, which held in Article 56 that "the transfer of an enemy vessel to a neutral flag effected after the outbreak of hostilities is void unless it is proved that such transfer was not made in order to evade the consequences to which an enemy vessel, as such, is exposed." The burden of proof of the bona fides of the transaction would lie with the individual or entity which effected the purchase and/or transfer of the vessel.[21]

Most of the 80 or so ships which had been reflagged after the passage of the new act only a few weeks earlier had been ships owned by American interests but registered with nations that were now belligerents, largely Great Britain. These owners, for obvious reasons, wanted to acquire the protection of American neutrality for their vessels, and changed their registration accordingly.[22] However, when a proposal was presented to the

American authorities for a German-owned ship to change her registry to an American-owned company which had German ties, that was an entirely different question. During these high-level deliberations over the future of the *Alexandria* the British announced that, while each case would be treated on its own merits, their general policy would be that German ships reflagged as American would be stopped on the high seas if they were suspected of carrying contraband cargo or if their new registry was not demonstrably a bona fide change of national interest.[23]

Although ship registration was a function of the newly independent and untested Department of Commerce under William C. Redfield, the importance of this issue mandated that the leadership of the entire administration be a part of the decision. The key players in Washington who shared in the resolution of this problem were not noted for their ability to make forceful, tough, and clear-headed decisions. President Woodrow Wilson, Secretary of State William Jennings Bryan, and Secretary of the Navy Josephus Daniels were men of peace, but were widely regarded as a bit fuzzy in their thinking on military matters. Earlier in 1914, they had delayed making decisions, and then made unwise decisions, regarding policy in Mexico, particularly at Vera Cruz. Now, after several weeks of vacillation, agreement was reached within the Wilson administration that the change of registration of the *Alexandria* should not be denied, absent any compelling reason to the contrary. As a result, the ship was formally registered as the American-flag *Sacramento* on October 8, 1914, and the customs officers in San Francisco reluctantly issued the necessary clearance papers. This registration decision eventually opened a Pandora's Box that would present the federal government with millions of dollars in legal costs, and would affect the lives of dozens of people.

On about the same date, even though there was still a detachment of American sailors on board, a German radio officer, Gustave Traub, surreptitiously came on board the *Sacramento* and stowed away, waiting for her departure.[24] This was the same man who had boarded the *Mazatlan* at San Pedro, and had helped to supervise the loading of coal aboard the *Leipzig* at Guaymas. His covert action in stowing away was relatively easy to carry out, even in the presence of the guard, because of the constant coming and going of various people in connection with the loading and crewing of the ship. This act was the first of a number of bizarre personnel transactions that were to occur during the final days while the ship was in San Francisco Bay.

The lengthy time consumed in the re-registration process and the newspaper coverage of the controversy, as well as the unique requirements imposed upon prospective crewmen, combined to make it difficult for the owners of the *Sacramento* to put together a crew for the proposed voyage to Valparaiso. It was eventually necessary to employ a shipping master—a more civilized twentieth-century version of a crimp—and a crew of runners to round up the requisite crewmen from the traditional haunts of merchant seamen in San Francisco.[25]

To appreciate more fully the *Sacramento* affair it is helpful to know as much as possible about the composition of the crew that was finally assembled, for two reasons. First, many of these men would scatter during the ship's subsequent lengthy detention in Valparaiso, their feelings and even their identities lost forever to journalists and historians, making it necessary to speculate in their absence about how the ship was operated during her brief and notorious career as an American steamer. Second, and more important, the world would soon wonder how any American seaman could serve voluntarily aboard a ship that was involved in such international chicanery. Knowing something about the crew may help supply at least reasonable conjectures in lieu of definitive answers to these questions.

As required by law, all the officers signing aboard the ship were citizens of the United States. At one point in the adoption of the recent federal legislation which authorized the re-registration of foreign ships under the American flag, it was proposed that the officers of foreign ships be allowed to serve on such re-flagged vessels. In fact, this discussion had led to several of the officers from the *Alexandria* hurriedly taking the examination for licensure as American mates and engineers.[26] However, when the legislation was finally signed into law it did not contain this provision, making it necessary to recruit a new set of officers for the ship.

Among the deck officers who joined the crew of the *Sacramento*, all of whom were naturalized citizens, the chief mate was originally from Finland, while the second and third mates were each from Denmark. The engineers came from somewhat more diverse backgrounds; the chief and second assistant engineer were native-born Americans, while the first assistant was from France and the third was from Sweden.[27]

At this point in maritime history, American steamship companies were free to use foreign crews on their ships. None of the unlicensed personnel in the deck department of the *Sacramento* was native-born. Two of the four Norwegian-born quartermasters were naturalized citizens and two were not. Similarly, among the able seamen, three were from Denmark and were not naturalized, while one was from Germany and one was from Norway, both of whom were naturalized American citizens.[28]

Among the rated personnel in the engine department, one oiler was from Ireland and naturalized, while the other was a native-born American. Among the firemen, two were native born, while the rest, none of whom was naturalized, were from Chile (3), Mexico (2), Spain (2), Ecuador, Peru, and Switzerland. On the long list of coal passers, two were native born, one was from England and naturalized, and the rest, all without American citizenship, were from Spain (2), San Salvador, Chile, and Holland.[29]

The small steward's department was about half German, and the rest Scandinavian and Mexican. Counting all three departments, fifteen different countries of origin, in addition to the United States, were represented in the 48-man crew, fully half of whom were not citizens of the United States. Only six of the crew were native-born citizens. Curiously, the captain would later sign a crew list that indicated that the entire crew was made up of citizens or subjects of the United States,[30] even though there were German citizens in the crew.

This analysis is not intended to suggest any grounds for disloyalty on the part of the crew. Indeed, this group was probably fairly typical of the kind of pick-up crew to be obtained in a cosmopolitan port such as San Francisco at that time. The problem created by the diversity of the crew came later as American authorities tried to find someone who had sailed on the ship, had returned to the United States, and could describe in reasonably good English what went on. Most of the information that was eventually obtained came from two of the engineers, one native born and one naturalized. These men had originally been taken off other ships belonging to the firm of Swayne & Hoyt and ordered aboard the *Sacramento*, an interesting development that pointed up the relationship of this steamship company to the newly-formed Northern and Southern Steamship Company.[31]

The 48-man crew of the *Sacramento* seemed unusually large for a freighter of that era. One explanation lies in the Shipping Articles signed between the master and the crew on October 14, 1914. In addition to the standard boiler-plate language and the destination—which read "Valparaiso, Chile, and return to San Francisco for final discharge for a term of time not exceeding six months"—another stipulation appeared on the contract. That stipulation read: "Crew to load and discharge all cargo and ballast if required by the Master." That requirement goes a long way in explaining why there were nine seamen in the deck department, plus twelve firemen and eight coal passers in the engine department. Furthermore, the crew was unusually young for a merchant ship of that era, with very few men as old as forty, a circumstance which would be beneficial later when it came time to shift the cargo about.

Signing the articles as master was John F. Jacobson, recently a captain of a coasting steamer, who had replaced the German captain M. Schulz who had brought the ship from Hamburg to San Francisco. However, after the articles were signed, another master was chosen by the company. This change was permitted under the articles by the phrase "or whoever shall go for Master" in the text of the agreement. In addition, five men listed on the roster of the original articles "failed to join," in the language of the Shipping Commissioner in whose presence the document was signed. Conspicuous among the absentees was the chief mate, a Norwegian named Johanson who was replaced by a man of Finnish extraction, Edmund Johnson.

The last-minute replacement for the master was Theodore A. Anderson, about whom little was known. Reportedly, he had worked as a pilot for the Kosmos Line on Puget Sound, so he appeared to have been hand-picked by management as a substitute about whom any reluctant crewmen would have little information.[32] The final changes in the crew, as we shall see, were made while the ship was literally on her way to sea.

Among the polyglot names listed on the articles were several crewmen of particular interest: those German citizens who as former members of the crew of the *Alexandria* had stayed aboard. Three of these men were former department heads on the ship. One was signed on as an "advising engineer," a non-existent position on American merchant ships; this man was Adolph Wimmel who had been chief engineer during the ship's German-flag days. Another was Benno Klocke, the purser, who had previously been chief mate and who was reportedly a reserve officer in the German Navy. Later, the unique role of these two men aboard the *Sacramento* would emerge clearly. In addition, Conrad Schule in the steward's department had been chief steward in the German crew, and one other man in the steward's department was also from that crew. Thus, there were four German nationals in the new crew, plus Traub, the stowaway who waited in the hold.[33]

At the time that the crew signed aboard, nothing was said about the possibility of the ship supplying coal to German warships. Merchant seamen of that era were singularly independent, keeping largely to themselves, and it is unlikely, given the number of languages spoken aboard, that there was much mutual speculation among the crew members at this time about the ultimate destination of the ship. Benjamin Tracey, the chief engineer and at age 51 the oldest man in the crew, acknowledged later that he knew something about the *Mazatlan* case, and thought that the *Sacramento* might be doing something similar. Concerning the cargo of coal, he said, "I thought it would go to Valparaiso, and then be transferred to some other boat and taken to the fleet."[34] Others in the crew may have felt somewhat uneasy signing on a ship which had been identified as a "hoodoo" by a local newspaper, but a job was a job in those days before seamen had many rights. Besides, Valparaiso was a pleasant enough place in the springtime to spend a couple of weeks discharging and loading. In fact, William Kooiman, in his book about the ships of Grace Line for whom he sailed as purser for many years, says "Valparaiso was easily everyone's favorite port .. . . A number of cabarets, bars and small hotels in the older port section comprised the seamen's quarter, almost heavily patronized and well known by mariners the world over."[35]

Consequently, no fiscal incentives were utilized in rounding up the crew. Peter Madison, the first engineer, recalled that in being pulled off another Swayne & Hoyt ship on which he was due to sail he had received no additional compensation for his trouble.[36] Wages for the crew ranged from $165 a month for the chief engineer down to $25 for the lowest ratings in the steward's department. In general, the engineering officers were paid somewhat more than their counterparts in the deck department.[37]

The departure of the ship was clouded in delay and in mystery. The ship had been loaded and ready to go for two weeks, and the change of registration was now almost a week old. The Navy had removed the armed guard, but the steamship company, which had waited until just before sailing to convene the crew for signing the articles, had still not filled all the vacancies. Nor had clearance been granted by customs officials. The logbook of the ship, normally a reliable source of information (but later to be highly suspect in the case of the *Sacramento*), indicated the following sequence of events, as paraphrased and condensed:

Wednesday, October 14, 1914: 10:45 a. m., ships articles signed; 10:00 p. m., chief mate signed, took on stores until midnight.

Thursday, October 15, 1914: 12:30 a. m., customs officers ashore; 4:45 a. m., weighed anchor, proceeded to sea; 7:30 a. m., dropped anchor; 8:30 a. m., weighed anchor, proceeded to sea; 10:45 a. m., returned from sea, anchored, captain went ashore; 2:30 p. m., captain returned, firemen signed articles; 3:15 p. m., weighed anchor, proceeded to sea in foggy weather; 5:10, dropped pilot.[38]

The second assistant engineer, Peter Madison, later recalled that a meeting with the crew was held at midnight on the sailing day at which a "United States judge" asked if any of the crew were agents of the German government or any other government, to which everyone replied no. It was only after this meeting that clearance was granted to the vessel at about 1 a. m. on the 15th of October.[39]

Madison also indicated that the initial pre-dawn departure was definitely an attempt to go to sea, but that the ship "broke down" off the headlands, and was forced to return.[40] This explanation would certainly account for the two hours and forty-five minutes spent between first weighing anchor and anchoring again. During the time that the ship was at anchor near Alcatraz with what was subsequently identified as boiler trouble, customs officials became suspicious of the reason for the delay. When the ship finally left, her path was blocked by the revenue cutter *Hartley* inside the Golden Gate. Only after the captain convinced the Deputy Collector of Customs, C. L. Brown, that the delay resulted from a legitimate engineering problem was the ship allowed to proceed. During the time spent at anchor which had worried the customs official, three additional crewmen decided to leave the ship and their replacements came aboard. Those who departed at the last moment were in addition to the radio officer.

Madison recalled that the American radio officer was sent ashore by boat during the engine trouble which had stopped the ship. This man, Frank Arnberger, had been brought aboard after the articles were signed on the 14th, even though the radio was still sealed by the American authorities. It is not clear if those authorities had decreed that the ship should make the entire trip without a radio; such an action could have jeopardized the safety of the ship unless an understanding existed that the seal could be broken in case of trouble.

Line 45 on the Shipping Articles was apparently set aside for a wireless operator inasmuch as the designation "W. O." appeared in the column of ratings, but no name was ever entered on that line. It is likely that the radio officer Arnberger had never signed the articles, but it is clear that he did leave the ship at the last moment. The first assistant engineer recalled that several Swayne & Hoyt officials came aboard in the channel during the time the engines were inoperative, and that the radio officer went ashore with some of them. The only explanation given to the crew was that the man had only a second-class, rather than a first-class, radiotelegraph license—a fatuous explanation that expected the hearer to believe that the lack of an operator was acceptable to the company, but an under-qualified operator was not.[41]

Newspaper accounts tell a different story, indicating that the federal official in charge of radio standards at San Francisco, Ellery W. Stone, initially wanted Arnberger removed from the ship because he did not have the minimum second-class license which was required. The ship's owners, however, pointed out to the inspector that he was confused about the identity of the ship which, while on a foreign voyage, required no operator at all.[42] If this were the case, it seems odd that the man had been hired after the signing of the articles, and then let go.

With the dropping of the pilot in the fog and gloom of late afternoon on October 15, 1914, the remarkable seagoing odyssey of the steamer *Sacramento* had now begun. Under the leadership of a captain and a chief mate who had been aboard no more than 24 hours, the manipulative guidance of a former chief engineer and chief mate of the ship from her days under the German flag, and the contacts with other ships and the outside world to be provided by a stowaway German radio officer, the naturalized American ship was assured a memorable voyage.

CHAPTER SIX

THE *SACRAMENTO* GOES SOUTH

The record of the first and only voyage of the SS *Sacramento* of the American firm called Northern and Southern Steamship Company is preserved in the log kept by the chief mate, supplemented by additional information provided by the chief and first assistant engineer of the ship in testimony in subsequent court cases.

The log that has been preserved is not the official log of the ship in the form prescribed by, and turned back into, the Shipping Commissioner. Instead it is on a standard form available at a ship chandler's, and identified as a first officer's log. Unlike modern practice, this log does not contained signed entries, either by the individual watch officers or by the chief mate or captain. In the case of the *Sacramento*, however, this chief mate's log, fictitious as it might be in places, was apparently the only record which could be retrieved by the American consul in Valparaiso and returned to the United States. The log was kept by Edmund Johnson, the replacement chief mate who came on board after the original ceremony of signing the ship's articles.[1]

Actually there are two such logs extant, one written in three different hands corresponding to the watch officers, and the other written in a single hand as if it were a summary version. The entries are similar, but not identical. One seems to stop after the ship had visited Mas Afuera Island and is signed, in perhaps a gesture of finality, by Edmund Johnson, while the other continues for at least another year after the ship arrived at Valparaiso, after which it was written in several different hands.

According to the second page of these logs, the day of October 16, 1914, dawned clear with light breezes as the *Sacramento* moved south on a course well off-shore from the normal trackline used by steamers along the California course. For the first 36 hours the magnetic course was S 10° W, at the end of which time the ship was 300 miles west of San Diego, a clear indication that the ship did not want to encounter normal steamer traffic. Only then did the ship change course more to the east to accommodate the falling away of the North American coastline in that direction.

The navigational entries in the logs appear to be reasonably consistent during the first part of the voyage, but after the ship crossed the equator there are frequent inconsistencies between the courses steered, noon position, distance made good, etc. The trackline of the ship for almost two weeks was in a general southeasterly direction, remaining well offshore. The only deviation from that track appeared to be when the ship swung farther to the west to avoid coming too close to Clipperton Island, a French possession which was reportedly without any residents at that time. The ship crossed the equator well outside the Galapagos Islands, then came east of the 90th meridian for the first time before starting on a general southerly course, again well offshore.

Although the log shows that the ship's radio was not unsealed until the 4th of November, testimony of the engineers suggests that the radio was put into operation immediately. The stowaway radio operator, Gustave Traub, showed up on deck the first day out of San Francisco, and showed the broken seal to the chief engineer and any others who were interested. For the first few mornings of the voyage he provided press news, a typed-up summary of the news as received on the commercial channels available to the operator, but this practice soon ended. Perhaps those in charge of the ship did not want the crew to know too much about what was going on in the outside world.

The captain was obviously not in full command of the ship. Although not in a position to observe the bridge routine closely, Chief Engineer Tracey noticed that the supercargo, Benno Klocke, was frequently on the bridge for navigational sights at noon and other times, and appeared to be making the decisions relative to course changes and other such matters. He also seemed concerned with the cargo in the holds.

Although they had an "advising" engineer looking over their shoulder in the person of Adolph Wimmel, the ship's engineers experienced little interference since there was not a distinctly German, as opposed to an American, way to operate the engines. Inasmuch as all the instruction plates and signs in the engine room were in German, Wimmel actually was useful in translating that information for the American engineers.[2]

Several inexplicable delays at sea occurred. On October 19th the engines were stopped for an hour and a half, on the

23rd for two hours, on the 24th for four hours and 35 minutes, and on the 25th five hours and forty minutes. In none of these instances was there any explanation made in the log. The engineers were apparently not asked about these delays at the follow-up hearings at the end of the entire episode.

The only other recorded change of routine occurred on October 24, when the course was altered for about an hour, apparently to accommodate communication with another ship. The log noted only "Spoke the British barque *Crown of India* 11 h 30 m," and indicated a course change of 26 degrees during that time. This sailing ship was not shown in *Lloyds Register* to have a radio, so apparently the conversation was by hailing. Why the Germans directing the movements of the ship would want to abandon their furtive ways and speak to another ship is not clear, unless perhaps they were trying to get information about the ship which they could pass on to the cruisers out ahead. At the time, the *Sacramento* was about 150 miles off Clipperton Island, the closest approach to land on the entire trip.

One of the features of the trip that bothered the engineers was the fact that the ship operated without running lights. In wartime, ships of belligerent nations frequently run without lights, but neutrals not only carry lights but sometimes paint their national flag on the hull and even floodlight that flag. The *Sacramento*, however, acted not like a neutral but as a combatant ship. Madison, the first assistant engineer, protested to Johnson, the chief mate, about the lack of lights, but was told that it was useless to complain because he "had orders from Washington to sail without lights."[3]

The question of the ship's destination frequently came up in conversation in the dining saloon, with much of the speculation centering on how the coal would be delivered. Neither Captain Anderson nor Klocke, the purser-supercargo, offered any information during these discussions, but apparently Traub, the radio officer, eventually began to hint that the coal was going to the German fleet. Madison remembered that on the first of November the radio officer passed along the news of the Battle of Coronel with the loss of the "*Mammoth*," apparently a reference to the *Monmouth*, one of two British cruisers lost that day. Traub also volunteered the advice that the ship should stay away from that area.[4]

Although the chief mate's log shows no entry acknowledging receipt of any instructions to do so, on November 4th it indicated "ordered the purser to break seals on the wireless and endevor (sic) to communicate with our agents at Valparaiso as to conditions regarding the British cruisers along the coast." The radio, of course, had been in operation during the entire trip. On that same day the *Sacramento* sent the following message: "Have received order to proceed direct to Valparaiso not to communicate with the squadron but to await further orders through confidential agent after arrival at Valparaiso." The addressee was "Dk" and the sender was "Vr i."[5]

On the following day the *Sacramento* received this message from the German cruiser *Dresden*: "By order of the Commodore *San* (sic) *Sacramento* is not to proceed to Valparaiso but to the Island of Mas a Fuera (sic).[6] Commodore has sent SMS *Dresden* to meet *San Sacramento* to convey this order." The *Dresden* was not one of the German cruisers which had come across the Pacific from China; instead she had come around from the Atlantic in time to join the cruiser squadron, and to participate in the Battle of Coronel. The indicated destination, Mas Afuera, was an island in the Juan Fernandez group, 450 miles off the Chilean coast.

That same day the *Sacramento* replied to the *Dresden*: "As I have American crew, stop us with a shot across our bows according to the usual practice in wartime. Proceed with lights out. Position at 6 p. m., 26° 07' S 83° 01' W. Steering S by E 3/4 E, true." It was clear that the *Sacramento* was participating in the planning of her own "capture" by the *Dresden*, and that the event was going to be staged for the benefit of the American crewmen who were ignorant of what was going on. The cruiser responded quickly the same evening with the information that, "the meeting point is to be 29° 10' S 82° 10' W, 6th November, p. m."

The staged encounter ran a bit late. At 4:30 a. m. on the 7th one of the logs of the *Sacramento* contains this interesting entry: "Sighted a vessel 2 points abaft the beam, who overtook us and at 5:00 a. m. made out signal to stop. Two officers boarded, and informed us that the vessel was the German cruiser *Dresden* and asked to see the ship's papers, etc., after which they ordered us to proceed as directed." The other log book has a much briefer entry and does not name the warship.

It also shows a 45 minute period in the afternoon when the engines were stopped, an event not recorded in the first log.

Twenty-four hours later the island of Mas Afuera had been sighted, and within another three hours the *Sacramento* was anchored off the north-northwest side of the island. Here she found the German cruiser squadron, fresh from its victory at the Battle of Coronel. Immediately, the freighter opened her eight hatches and began to discharge coal into the bunkers of the German cruiser *Scharnhorst* which came alongside.

Over the next ten days, no less than nine German vessels, including five warships and their colliers, would receive coal and supplies from the *Sacramento*. The ship's log was not reticent in acknowledging that after the *Scharnhorst* came the cruisers *Gneisenau*, *Leipzig*, and *Dresden*, followed by the colliers *Santa Isabel*, *Baden*, and *Amasis*, the auxiliary cruiser *Prinz Eitel Friedrich*, and the small collier and naval auxiliary, *Titania*. Of the ships in the cruiser squadron, only *Nürnberg*, which had been a late arrival at the Battle of Coronel, failed to benefit directly from the efforts of the *Etappe* in San Francisco in reflagging the former *Alexandria*. Several other merchant steamers and sailing vessels were also at the island during this time, but did not take any coal or supplies from the *Sacramento*.

For the most part, the sailors on the German cruisers did the bulk of the work of coaling. The observant engineers on the *Sacramento* were interested to note the camaraderie that existed between the officers of the German cruisers and the Germans on their own ship, plus that of their deck officers as well. Madison noted that everything was business-like, with bills of lading being presented by the German officers for the coal to which their cruiser was entitled. Both German and English were spoken during these transactions. There was also plenty of social life, with German officers constantly aboard the *Sacramento*, having drinks with Captain Anderson, Benno Klocke, and Adolph Wimmel. The deck officers of the freighter also participated in the social drinking, but kept to themselves rather than trying to penetrate the in-group of Germans. The engineers were apparently not invited.[7]

From time to time it was necessary to shift anchorages to minimize the effect of the long Pacific swell on the coaling operations. The verdant setting ashore was attractive, but there was no opportunity for the seamen to enjoy it. Mas Afuera was the outermost of the Juan Fernandez Islands, and was still wooded from the ample precipitation which fell there. The island closer to the mainland, Mas a Tierra, had been largely cut over and no longer resembled the island described in Defoe's *Robinson Crusoe*, a title that was sometimes applied to that island. In contrast, the unpopulated Mas Afuera, rising to a height of more than 5,400 feet, remained the epitome of the island of south seas castaways, and was often referred to as Alexander Selkirk Island for the English freebooter who spent time here and was used as Defoe's inspiration and model.

Eventually this great rendezvous of ships ended, and Admiral von Spee with his squadron of five German cruisers headed south for the Straits of Magellan. The auxiliary cruiser *Prinz Eitel Friedrich*, a passenger liner armed only with guns taken from two German gunboats at Tsingtao, was left behind as being unsuited for major combat. Also, the supply ship *Titania* was scuttled as being too small and slow, a curious decision since she had just loaded coal from the *Sacramento*. Her sinking in Chilean territorial waters was soon to be regarded as a breach of neutrality by the authorities on the mainland, where Germany's once-assured popularity was waning with each passing day because of such acts.

Accompanying the naval squadron were the *Baden* and *Santa Isabel*, each of which would soon be sunk at the Battle of the Falkland Islands, along with four of the German cruisers. Another collier, the *Seydlitz*, which had been acquired by the squadron before reaching the Falkland Islands, would replace the *Amasis* which had remained in the Straits of Magellan. The *Seydlitz*, along with the cruiser *Dresden*, would survive the battle; the collier would be interned as a naval auxiliary when she tried to take refuge in Argentina, while the *Dresden* would escape to the west. En route, the cruiser would coal at Punta Arenas from the *Amasis* with a supply obtained from the American-flag *Minnesotan* before reaching the Pacific; eventually she would be scuttled by her crew at Mas Afuera to avoid capture by the British.

Returning to the post-Coronel milieu, it was now time for the *Sacramento* to face the music, to accept the consequences of what she had done. Although not mentioned in her log, she apparently had taken on board the crew of the large four-masted French barque *Valentine* which had been captured and brought into Mas Afuera.[8] With these men aboard and with no cargo in her holds the *Sacramento* came into Valparaiso on Saturday evening, November 20, 1914, 36 days out of San Francisco. The first log entry after dropping anchor suggests how things were shaping up for the crew: "No communication allowed from shore. Water police aboard guarding the ship. Wireless operator, purser, and supervising engineer ashore." Thus, the three Germans who had run the ship were allowed to go ashore, even though there were many questions that the local Chilean, American, and British authorities wanted answered.

The already terse log entries now became even more laconic, making it very difficult to know what was going on. The American vice consul, angry that the captain had reported to the Kosmos Line before reporting to him, immediately started an investigation, but cabled the Secretary of State for guidance. Apparently Captain Anderson eventually told the consul that the ship had been stopped by the *Dresden*, ordered to Mas Afuera where her cargo was taken from her, and then sent on her way. After this report was made, a token protest was filed by the owners of the ship, but there was no sense of indignation expressed by her owners or her captain that an American ship had been forcibly detained and her cargo, destined for a neutral nation, taken from her. In fact, the Kosmos Line office in Valparaiso made the entire incident sound quite routine. In a letter to Harold H. Ebey of the Kosmos Line in San Francisco, the resident agent in Valparaiso observed:

> *Sacramento* arrived here on the 20th November at 6 p. m. empty, since all her cargo had been taken by the German squadron cruising in these waters, by virtue of the "right of preemption." The master noted consular protest in order to protect the interest of his owners and we have been able to arrange with the owners of the cargo, the Compania de Tranvias Electricos de Valparaiso, that they will not claim against the steamer, but that they will lodge a claim against the German

> Government. The Commander in Chief of the
> German squadron, Vice Admiral Graf von Spee,
> extended a certificate to Captain Anderson
> leaving on record what had happened to ship
> and cargo. This certificate has been filed with
> the U. S. Consul at this place and will entitle
> the owners of the *Sacramento* to be
> compensated by the Imperial German
> Government for any prejudice caused by the
> incident referred to.[9]

The story initially sounded phony, to say the least, and the explanation by the German steamship company made it no less so. If events had happened the way the captain claimed, then both the United States and Chile had reason to make an international *cause celebre* out of the German behavior in the incident. If not, a serious unneutral act had obviously been committed by the American ship.

The *New York Times* editorialized on November 27 that it was likely that the "entire transaction of the transfer to the American flag and the clearance at the port of San Francisco was fraudulent and was carried out by German procurement for German war purposes." Nevertheless, it took the State Department several weeks to accept the possibility that the American authorities had been duped. In the meantime, Secretary of State William Jennings Bryan busied himself with such important matters as polite replies to earlier German protests about the treatment the *Mazatlan* and the *Sacramento* had received from the authorities in San Francisco.[10]

While Washington was reacting indifferently to these developments, American consul Aldis B. Easterling in Valparaiso kept the Department of State informed of what was going on. Ambassador Fletcher in Santiago also stayed in touch with the situation. On December 29 he informed the Secretary of State in a cablegram that "unless *Sacramento* leaves within twenty-four hours, as notified to do through the American Consulate this afternoon, both ship and crew will be interned. Consulate acting under the instructions of Department, November 30, 7 p. m., is holding ship's papers."[11]

At last the ship was under the supervision of someone besides the Germans, but she still was unable to control her own destiny. She could not leave without her papers which the American consul controlled, and if she did not leave immediately, internment by the Chileans would be the result.

Bryan responded promptly, but again appeared to pass the buck. "As circumstances of case appear to show that register was fraudulently obtained, Department of Commerce requests that Consul withhold ship's papers and refuse to discharge crew until further notice . . . . Department of Commerce would be pleased to see vessel and crew interned."[12]   Bryan invoked the name of the Department of Commerce, inasmuch as its maritime functions at that time included both the registration of vessels through the Bureau of Navigation and the shipping of seamen through the shipping commissioners. Overseas, all American shipping laws and regulations were enforced through the consuls; consequently the crewmen were dependent upon the American consul in Valparaiso for their discharge papers and return transportation home when the six months contract was up.

The Chilean government was not bluffing; even though the ship's log book characteristically showed no entry to that effect, the *Sacramento* was interned on or about December 30, 1914. There was, however, no indication that the crewmen were interned in the sense of having their movements restricted. As the justification for interning this merchant ship, the Chileans had their choice of at least two causes: rendering unneutral service, or serving as a naval auxiliary for a belligerent.

Now the ship settled into a long year of inactivity. During this time, the Chilean government exchanged a number of crisp notes with the German government about the violation of the Chilean neutrality which had occurred at Easter Island, Mas Afuera, and other locations. Upon the six-month anniversary of the signing of the articles, the crewmen of the *Sacramento* were released from their contract and sent home, at least those who were still together. It is not clear how they were paid, if indeed they were, during the interim.

A number of the crewmen chose not to be repatriated at this time, including the captain and his deck officers, and possibly some of the South American natives in the crew. Slightly less than half the crew returned on the *City of Para* when she arrived in San Francisco on June 9, 1915; this group included two of the engineers, the third mate, and 21 unlicensed crewmen.[13] Health problems had scattered the crew somewhat; one man had died in the hospital from the effects of a drinking bout, and there had been considerable other sickness which hospitalized several of the crew, including the captain who came down with typhoid fever. If and when another group of crewmen came home is not clear.

Logbook entries continued through most of 1915, with little information posted other than the weather. Some of the sparse entries suggest that the ship was slipping back into her Germanic ways; e. g., the "advising engineer" Adolph Wimmel had become first assistant engineer, shore support was provided by tugs of the Kosmos Line, and the new mate, a man named Normann who started keeping the log in mid-May, occasionally reverted to German in making entries. Since the ship had been interned by Chile, the American consulate no longer had much influence in what went on.

Finally, on November 15, 1915, a cryptic last log entry appeared: "Captain Cross came on board to take command over the ship." The standard ship registers show that the *Sacramento* was acquired eventually by a British firm in 1916. Her sellers, the Northern and Southern Steamship Company, received $765,000 for the ship or almost six times what they paid for her, with none of the money reverting to the Germans who had been her real owners.[14]

She would now start her rehabilitation into the ranks of respectable ships as the *Bayramento* for the Bay Steamship Company of London. Thus, the coming of "Captain Cross" may have been the beginning of her new life, as she took up the flag of the country in which she had been built as the *Alexandria* sixteen years earlier.

Back in San Francisco, the local authorities were beginning to awake from their complacency. By mid-1915 they would be alert enough to file the first formal charges against the large group of people who had been involved in the *Sacramento* scandal.

CHAPTER SEVEN

THE *OLSON & MAHONY* SCHEME

Even before the battle of Coronel had taken place, the San Francisco *Ettape* was readying another ship to follow the *Sacramento* south with supplies for the German cruiser squadron. Under the leadership of Korvettencapitän Wolfram von Knorr who had arrived in late September from his previous posting as naval attaché in Tokyo, the Germans were able to put together a remarkable new plan. This scheme was even more brazen than the earlier one in that the featured ship was, and always had been, an American vessel.

To a greater degree than in the *Sacramento* case, the story of this next vessel to achieve notoriety is obscured by a lack of comprehensive reports both in newspapers and in court documents. Accounts of this episode are fragmented, with a number of short items appearing about one person or one aspect of the story, around which it is necessary to weave the continuity that brings everything together. In this process, loose ends may appear, but for the most part the story that follows can be verified in its essentials.

The ship involved in this new scheme was the *Olson & Mahony*, a 1,497-ton steel-hulled coasting steamer built for and operated by the steamship company of the same name. This company, owned by Oliver J. Olson and Andrew F. Mahony, operated a fleet of small, mostly wooden, steam schooners which were in the lumber trade on the north coast of California. This prosaic service is not exactly the source one would expect a network of intrigue to draw upon in supplying warships at distant anchorages; perhaps this thought had occurred to the *Etappe* officials as they recognized how useful this ship could be to them because she was such an unlikely candidate for suspicion.

The *Olson & Mahony* was the showplace ship of the small steamship company, the acquisition of which had come as a result of a public stock offering which had been oversubscribed.[1] Built in 1907 at Wilmington, Delaware, she was 224 feet in overall length, with a beam of 41 feet and a depth of 21 feet. These dimensions made her somewhat larger than the *Titania* which had served as a supply ship for the German fleet in China and in the South Pacific before being scuttled at Mas Afuera. Although she was configured to carry as many as sixty passengers, the *Olson & Mahony* generally had worked as a freighter. Even though she was considered a west coast ship, she was actually registered in the port of New York.

Shortly after the story of the *Sacramento* became public when that ship arrived in Valparaiso on November 20, 1914, the British Ambassador to the United States, Cecil Spring-Rice, wrote to Secretary of State William Jennings Bryan, expressing his government's concern over an upcoming voyage of the new ship that was loading in San Francisco. He indicated that:

> His Majesty's Government have reliable information that some of the persons connected in the dealings of the *Sacramento* are now concerned in the *Olson and Mahony* vessel under the United States flag, which is due to sail on November 24 from San Francisco with Valparaiso as ostensible destination. These facts make it more than probable that this vessel, like the *Sacramento*, is also engaged in supplying German cruisers.
>
> Under these circumstances of gravest suspicion I have the honour to request that the *Olson and Mahony* may not be allowed to sail without a most careful and searching investigation on the part of the United States Government.[2]

For the most part, a strange indifference to reality existed at that moment within the U. S. State Department. Not only did William Jennings Bryan in December respond courteously to Germany on the question of the naval armed guard which had earlier been placed aboard the now-notorious *Sacramento* in San Francisco,[3] he had also sent a letter in response to a British inquiry, in which he pointed out that the Department of Justice of the United States had "failed to discover any facts in the case of the *Mazatlan* constituting a violation of the Federal penal laws."[4] Yet, in spite of his head-in-the-sand posture on these two widely-recognized swindles, someone in the State Department was able to get Bryan's attention on the *Olson & Mahony* case. On the day following receipt of the British letter,

Above, the greatest coup carried out jointly by the German consulate and a group of aggressive shipping men of San Francisco was in reflagging a former German freighter as the U. S.-flag *Sacramento*, and sending that ship with American coal to fuel the German cruiser squadron off the coast of Chile. Below, this view of the German supply ship *Titania* being scuttled off Mas Afuera shows the steep eastern slope of the island where the German cruisers rendezvoused and were coaled by the *Sacramento*.

S. S. Olson & Mahoney

Above, after the successful voyage of the *Sacramento*, the shipping conspirators tried again to supply the German cruisers by using the homely lumber ship, *Olson & Mahony*, but the venture was abandoned when American authorities became suspicious. Below, when the German-Hindu gun-running plot was being hatched, the schooner *Annie Larsen* was selected as a ship that could carry a cargo of arms without raising suspicions about the final destination of the weapons.

Bryan responded with a cautious, albeit buck-passing, letter indicating ". . . on the 23rd instant, this matter was brought to the attention of the Secretary of the Treasury for his appropriate action."[5] That official, William G. McAdoo within whose purview came U. S. Customs, was one of the more effective trouble-shooting officials of the administration of Woodrow Wilson who happened to be his father-in-law, so the proper wheels may have been set in motion to counter the German abuse of the neutrality laws.

It should be noted that, inasmuch as similar efforts were being made on the east coast to supply the coal and other needs of German warships through American ships, public awareness of the role of German diplomats in these clandestine transactions was growing, although the major exposes of German espionage in this country had not yet occurred. Nevertheless, the government's tolerant posture toward violations of neutrality had permitted these cargo shipments to continue well beyond the point of initial disclosure. Although there were considerably more ships, both German and American, on the east coast with which to participate in such furtive activities, somehow the west coast became the center of the most resourceful and innovative shipping schemes concocted by the *Etappen*—even though German naval histories later complained about the strictness of the west coast officials.

Control of the *Olson & Mahony* had been acquired by the Germans in the San Francisco *Etappe* under a charter arranged by two local steamship agents, Robert Capelle and Joseph L. Bley, whose names would figure prominently in several of the neutrality frauds which were now beginning to surface in connection with the earlier coal shipments.[6] At the beginning of the war, Capelle was the San Francisco agent for the North German Lloyd Steamship Company, and was an associate of Fred Jebsen, the German ship owner who was an integral part of the *Etappe* in the Bay Area. Bley was the co-owner and active partner in the customs house brokerage firm of C. D. Bunker & Company, which had been the consignors of the coal in the *Sacramento* case. He, too, was an associate of the notorious Fred Jebsen.

Although both men were well known in shipping circles, each chose to use an alias in conducting his extra-legal activities. To the office staff of C. D. Bunker and in the office of Louis T. Hengstler who was attorney for the German consulate, Capelle was known as Scott. Similarly, Bley was known in the office of Fred Jebsen as Dr. Ross. The use of these false names would later prove awkward to explain.[7]

The company which chartered the *Olson & Mahony* was the Golden Gate Transport Company, owned by two brothers, George and James Flood. The shipment to be carried in this vessel to Valparaiso consisted of a large amount of foodstuffs, which the newspapers promptly characterized as a cargo of sauerkraut. The money for the purchase of this cargo was furnished by the German government through the shipping agency of Oelrichs & Co. of New York which was handling the affairs of a number of German ships interned in New York as naval auxiliaries. The funds in the form of two checks totaling $250,000 were deposited by Capelle in his name as trustee on September 22, 1914, and November 10, 1914, at the Anglo London & Paris National Bank in San Francisco.

In order to conceal the German connection with the cargo, Capelle used one of his employees, a man named Hall, to deposit additional checks from Baron von Schack, the German vice consul in San Francisco, and from other German sources, checks aggregating about $140,000. Hall was asked to adopt the first name of Arthur, rather than his real name of Maurice, in carrying out these transactions. Hall deposited these checks, and then made the rounds of the various concerns which had supplied the components of the cargo, writing checks and dispensing large amounts of cash in payment of the bills they had submitted.[8] Hall, incidentally, was also the Turkish consul in San Francisco, but there is no indication that his actions made use of that position in any way.

Although problems remained in getting the necessary clearance from customs for a trip to Valparaiso on the heels of the *Mazatlan* and *Sacramento* affairs, the Golden Gate Transport Company in mid-November went ahead with the loading of the ship. In justifying their request for clearance, the charterers of the *Olson & Mahony* indicated to port authorities that one reason for sending the ship to Valparaiso was to pick up a valuable return cargo in the form of goods destined for the United States which were stranded aboard two Kosmos Line ships that dared not leave Chilean ports. The same argument had been used earlier in the case of the *Sacramento*.

When the loading was complete, the ship spent about ten days at anchor waiting for the clearance to be granted, with the revenue cutter *McCullough* anchored nearby. During this time the local Collector of Customs, John O. Davis, became aware that another possible fraud was in the works; he was therefore relieved when a directive from Washington ordered him to deny the clearance.[9]

Local federal authorities then convened a grand jury to investigate what had been taking place. This grand jury began by looking at the financial transactions; early in its deliberations it voted a presentment to the District Court, asking that George F. Herr, the bank cashier who had accepted the German checks on deposit, be cited for not providing information on the source of the deposits that funded the purchases.[10] After being jailed briefly, Herr acknowledged that the man known as Hall had deposited $139,000 for that purpose.[11]

During the grand jury hearings, the fact emerged that the foodstuffs and other provisions on board the *Olson & Mahony* as cargo were shipped by the San Francisco wholesale grocery house of Haas and Company, and were consigned to A. H. Foelsch & Co. of Valparaiso. William Haas, the president of the grocery company, took the fifth amendment when asked with whom he had dealt when the order was filled. Payment for the goods, he acknowledged, was made by a Mr. Hall, about whom Haas professed to have no further information. This man was apparently that employee of Robert Capelle who was used as a front for disbursing the German funds. The man who had originally placed the order, and whom Haas refused to name, was later identified as a Frederick Williams, presumably an assumed name, who had come up from Valparaiso to order the provisions.[12]

On December 2nd, after facing both an inquiry by the Collector of Customs and the grand jury investigation, and after having shelled out $210 a day in charter costs to her owners which represented costly demurrage while the ship swung at anchor, the Flood Brothers gave up on their efforts to send the *Olson & Mahony* to Valparaiso. Unable to find another place to ship their cargo of foodstuffs, they withdrew their application for clearance, and offloaded the ship. Reports differ on the subsequent distribution of the cargo; some indicate that the provisions were distributed to Germans interned on the west coast,[13] but others indicate that at least a portion of it went to the interned German gunboat *Cormoran* at Guam.[14] A spokesman for the consignees in Valparaiso said that the perishable part of the cargo was reshipped by rail to New York for further transportation to Chile.[15] This spokesman, along with those for the Flood Brothers and Haas & Company, insisted that the original shipment was a legitimate and innocuous merchandise transaction, and that the federal government had over-reacted to it.

Some evidence supports this position. The federal authorities had described the cargo as being just the sort of supplies a German warship would need: sauerkraut, beer, woolen sweaters, potatoes, flour, baking powder, etc.[16] However, it would not take much imagination to visualize the utilization of those supplies by civilians at hundreds of ports in the world. If one ignored the suspicious nature of the secrecy employed by the various people through whom the purchase of the cargo was made, a reasonable case could have been made for the bona fide nature of this export transaction which was otherwise legal.

The officers of the firm of Olson & Mahony, still insisting that they had done nothing wrong, announced that their steamer *Oliver J. Olson* would be dispatched to pick up the lucrative Kosmos Line cargoes which they claimed had been the initial attraction in sending ships to Chile.[17] This ship did go as far south as Arica and Tocopilla in northern Chile early in 1915, returning to New Orleans, but it is not clear whether the cargo she found was from one of the Kosmos Line ships. After abandoning their efforts to salvage the voyage of the *Olson & Mahony* to Valparaiso, the Flood brothers sent that ship north to Grays Harbor for a cargo, most likely lumber, which she took to the east coast through the Panama Canal.[18] Thus, the active role of this steamer in supplying German warships ended before it ever began.

By this time, however, the loss of the ship's capability meant little to the *Etappe* in San Francisco because the provisioning requirements of German warships in the Pacific had declined markedly. On December 8, 1914, the British soundly defeated the German cruiser squadron at the Falkland Islands, with only the *Dresden* escaping. That ship survived three more months in virtual hiding before she was hunted down at the Juan Fernandez Islands where the German cruisers had held their last rendezvous before heading into the Atlantic. There in March, 1915, her crew scuttled her to avoid capture.

With the passing of the *Dresden* there was virtually nothing left of a German fleet in the Pacific to be supplied out of San Francisco. This situation had been compounded when the gunboat *Geier* and the auxiliary cruiser *Cormoran* were interned at Honolulu and Guam, respectively, and the auxiliary cruiser *Prinz Eitel Friedrich*, a survivor of the great rendezvous at Mas Afuera, went around into the Atlantic, eventually to be interned at Newport News, Virginia.

The Flood brothers, meantime, did not give up on the *Olson & Mahony* without a fight. They instituted a suit against the Collector of Customs for $107,200, representing the losses they had sustained when the vessel was refused clearance.[19] The suit was successfully defended by the United States, with federal judge William C. Van Fleet ruling that the company had neither completed nor complied with the clearance procedures, which gave it no basis for a claim.[20] After this ruling, indictments were returned against those people responsible for the false statements in the application for clearance.

American authorities now had reason to be pleased in that progress was at last being made in determining what was acceptable commercial activity for the steamship companies of a neutral nation. For the first time, a fraud against the United States by the profit-minded shipping community in San Francisco had been nipped in the bud. Participants had been named, several of whom had ties to the earlier cases. Furthermore, the wheels of justice, which grind so notoriously slow, had at least been set in motion. Thus, the *Olson & Mahony* case became the watershed action for the federal authorities in dealing with the shipping conspiracies of 1914-15.

In other respects, however, it was the least interesting of all the neutrality frauds. Nothing had happened; no ship had sailed, and no men were caught up in conflict with the sea or with each other. There were neither heroes nor villains associated with the aborted voyage, and the ship had acquired none of the mystery and notoriety which surrounded the other ships which were a part of the swindles and subterfuges carried out by the Germans during the first year of the war. Perhaps what the entire effort lacked was the touch of the master maritime plotter, Fred Jebsen.

For the Germans, the episode had turned out unsatisfactorily, but not badly. The members of the *Etappe* in San Francisco certainly had not pulled off the great coup that had been theirs in the *Mazatlan* and *Sacramento* ventures, but neither had they encountered disaster. Their organization was still in place, although now, with no further requirement to support a cruiser squadron, they were forced to re-orient their efforts toward providing sustenance to other aspects of the German war effort, including gun-running and sabotage.

The momentum, however, was now shifting to the American authorities who were beginning to anticipate German movements. But before any real results were achieved in uncovering and punishing criminal behavior in the three cases already pending—the two coal shipments and now the *Olson & Mahony*—there would be one more shipping scandal engineered by the incongruous group of conspirators in San Francisco. This bold venture could easily have been prevented at the outset and at several points during its development, but inexplicably it was not. The resultant episode turned out to be the strangest one of all.

CHAPTER EIGHT

THE GERMAN-HINDU CONSPIRACY:
THE *ANNIE LARSEN*

Early in 1915, after the circumstances of the various attempts at supplying the German cruisers through San Francisco-based ships had become known, one additional effort to help the German cause was made jointly by the *Etappe* and American shipping interests. This action was taken before the American authorities had implemented any punitive action in response to the earlier attempts. Before turning to this final cargo conspiracy, however, it will be useful to consider some of the other aggressive actions which were being instituted at the same time by the German consulate in San Francisco.

After the *Olson & Mahony* adventure had ended in a stalemate, the staff of the consulate began to think about other kinds of mischief which they could sponsor in addition to the shipping conspiracies. Sabotage was a natural choice, although with the United States solidly neutral such activities would have to be directed at other countries or against American exports to allied nations.

Canada was a particularly appealing target. When consul Franz Bopp returned from Germany to his post in San Francisco in March, 1915, he brought with him money and instructions for implementing a campaign of sabotage against railways and other transportation facilities in western Canada. Bopp's initial efforts in this direction, however, proved to be much more amateurish than were any of the cargo plots.

This German ineffectiveness was well illustrated in the case of the Dutchman with a British passport, J. F. Van Koolbergen, who volunteered to help the Kaiser's cause. This man, in the double-agent tradition, met with Wilhelm von Brincken from the consulate, and ultimately agreed to blow up a tunnel on the Canadian Pacific Railway in British Columbia for a fee of $3,000. He then visited the British consul in San Francisco, A. Carnegie Ross, and described the plan to him. Ross passed the information along to his government which worked out a scheme to have newspapers in Vancouver carry a story that the tunnel had collapsed. Citing this newspaper story as proof, the Dutchman eventually collected most of his fee from the Germans at the consulate. Both Van Koolbergen and his German employers were satisfied with the transaction, but the

British were disappointed in that no tangible wrongdoing by the Germans could be proven since nothing had really happened to the tunnel.

Nevertheless, the unsuspecting Germans went ahead with new plans. Von Brincken was given the responsibility for recruiting agents in the United States to carry out further sabotage in Canada and the Northwest. The military attaché soon came in contact with Charles C. Crowley who had once been head detective for the Southern Pacific Railroad, but had since been fired by the company. The disgruntled detective was anxious to make some of the good money paid by the Germans, so he joined their sabotage squad as an agent. He was even provided an office and a secretary.

Crowley's first task was to recruit additional help to conduct more acts of sabotage. The detective located Louis J. Smith, an American of German descent, who had been employed in the Hercules Powder plant across the bay at Pinole but, like Crowley, had recently been fired. Through his contacts at the plant, Smith was soon able to learn that gunpowder from the plant was to be shipped to Russia, one of the allies. The explosives were to be shipped to Tacoma, Washington, for transshipment to Vladivostok, the terminus for the trans-Siberian railroad.

Recognizing a good opportunity, von Brincken sent Crowley and Smith to Tacoma to place bombs aboard the *Hazel Dollar* and three other merchant ships which were scheduled to load the powder. After arriving in Puget Sound, Smith, under the name of Walter Weaver, obtained dynamite and fuses for this project from the local DuPont Powder Works.

On May 30, 1915, Tacoma and Seattle were jarred by an enormous explosion. The barge load of powder from Hercules had disappeared in a blinding flash. An immediate investigation disclosed Smith's purchase of the powder and fuses, which eventually led to his arrest. However, the case was circumstantial, and when he was brought to trial a skilled defense lawyer was able to get him acquitted. The case was never solved.

Although the bombing had raised the specter of a powerful German sabotage network, Bopp and von Brincken were worried about the outcome of the enterprise. They hustled Smith and Crowley out of Seattle, sending them to Detroit to carry out further sabotage on Canadian railroads. The saboteurs soon wised up; this time they did nothing, but eventually returned to San Francisco to collect their fee for blowing up an non-existent train. Smith was sent back to Detroit for further undercover operations.

However, Smith soon began to think that he was in danger from the Germans because he knew too much. In October, 1915, he went to the U. S. Attorney in Detroit and told his story. The Department of Justice was delighted to have the information necessary to proceed against the German consular officials in San Francisco. In 1916 the federal authorities put together the case of U. S. v. BOPP et al, a significant indictment since it charged criminal acts by German diplomatic personnel for the first time in a case involving the violation of American neutrality. That case hung over the heads of the consular officials in San Francisco as the other cases in which they had played a role began to unfold during and after 1916.

Parallel to the sabotage activity in 1915 had been the final German effort in the west coast cargo conspiracies. These actions involved some of the same die-hard consular employees and German sympathizers who had been part of the previous incidents, but it also brought a new set of people into the conspiracies: a nationalist group from the Asian continent with a grudge against the British. This plot also represented an attempt to deliver supplies, not to a German ship, but to a distant land where conceivably some support for the German cause could be found.

The plot that developed has been called the "German-Hindu Conspiracy," although it appeared to be a political movement involving native people of the Dominion of India who were seeking independence from Great Britain, rather than a movement unique to Hindus as a religious group. In fact, Sikhs were prominent in the leadership of the group, and Moslems were also included. Perhaps the designation Hindu was chosen as the most recognizable and acceptable term for residents of India, to avoid using the term Indian which, of course, in the United States has a completely different connotation.

Indian independence activities all over the world were well known prior to the outbreak of the World War. These efforts were brought into sharp focus in 1913 when an Indian national named Har Dayal who was a graduate student at the University of California at Berkeley founded the Ghadar Party. Dayal had apparently been a lecturer at Stanford University, but had been dismissed because of his extreme political views.[1]

The objectives of the movement were defined in a document called the Ghadar Extracts, published in Urdu and other Indian languages, which identified the methods of the party as assassination and bombings. The primary objective of the Indian revolutionaries in the United States was to promote an insurrection in their homeland that would ultimately lead to India's independence from Great Britain. The goals of the movement were understandable enough in a country which had won its independence from Great Britain, but the doctrines of violence and terrorism contained in its literature disturbed American authorities. Consequently, Dayal was arrested and detained for deportation as an undesirable alien. However, he managed to escape confinement and to flee the country.

When he was subsequently free abroad, Dayal was persuaded by German agents to go to Berlin. There, the Secretary for Foreign Affairs, Arthur Zimmermann, later to be notorious for his note to the Mexican government, met with the deportee and other representatives from the Indian independence movement. Quickly the German government sensed how useful this cause might be to the country's war goals. If this group could foment trouble in India, Great Britain would be forced to commit additional troops there, troops that might otherwise be used in Europe. This possibility, coupled with the presence of a large number of Indian militants in the San Francisco Bay area, was the rationale for the newest German shipping adventure.

This episode involved two small, old, and rather ordinary vessels. One was the well-known 376-ton three-masted schooner *Annie Larsen*, built of yellow fir by Hall Brothers in 1881 for James Tuft of San Francisco. The other ship was the aging Standard Oil tanker *Maverick* of 1,560 tons, dating from 1890. These two ships were thrown together in a bizarre scheme of gun-running that smacked of the old days of the filibusters, those men who invaded other countries with the hopes of toppling governments. After a brief review of the essence of this plot, the two ships will be considered separately in the next several chapters inasmuch they operated as separate entities throughout the full course of the conspiracy.

The *Annie Larsen* had been utilized in the workaday coastwise lumber trade by Olson & Mahony, the same company whose namesake ship received so much notoriety in the fall of 1914. She had also made several offshore voyages to Pacific Islands with lumber cargoes. Early in 1915 she was placed under time charter for $1,250 a month by H. Martinez & Company, a San Diego customs broker acting on behalf of the German government. The time frame of the charter was indefinite, but a clause in the document indicated that upon expiration of the charter the vessel would be returned to her owners in the Pacific Northwest.[2]

In another of those complicated transactions designed to make it difficult for anyone to trace, the $14,000 to finance the charter was deposited in a San Francisco bank by a heavily veiled woman who pulled the money in cash from the muff she carried. She identified herself to the bank as Jean Fisher of Vancouver, B. C., but her true identify and residence was subsequently never discovered.[3] However, federal authorities suspected that she was Margaret Cornell, an assistant to Charles C. Crowley, the detective who would soon figure in the plot hatched by the German consulate in San Francisco to bomb the ships in Puget Sound, an act for which both he and his assistant were eventually indicted and convicted.

This money deposited by "Jean Fisher" was placed in two different accounts of the German consulate in equal amounts of $7,000 each.[4] The mysterious woman also requested that the funds be wired to J. Claude Hizar, an attorney in San Diego who had once served as city attorney for the affluent community of Coronado, and now as a reserve officer was on active duty as a paymaster in the Navy aboard the USS *San Diego*, flagship of the Pacific Fleet. By the time that Hizar received the money, another $5,000 had inexplicably been added to it.

Although Hizar was a prominent figure in San Diego, he had strong German connections as well as maritime contacts. He had been employed by the German consulate the previous year in connection with the Alamo affair, the placing of a German radio station in western Mexico in the fall of 1914. Following a meeting with Jebsen and von Schack early in January, 1915, he seems to have played the leading role in bringing together the various people in San Diego who readied the *Annie Larsen* for her role in this venture.[5]

The cargo transaction was even more complex than lining up the vessel had been. The overall plan called for the *Annie Larsen* to proceed to San Diego where a cargo of surplus U. S. Army rifles, pistols, and ammunition, all at least 25 years old, would be taken aboard. These arms were part of a large stock assembled in New York by a representative of the Krupp munitions works, Captain Hans Tauscher.[6] Some sources suggest that responsibility for a part of this stock was turned over to an Indian, Heramba Lai Gupta, who had been sent to the United States where he was provided with a substantial amount of money by the German Ambassador to this country, Count Johann Heinrich von Bernstorff.[7] However, Germans seemed to have conceived and executed the entire transaction. As one historian of the Ghadar movement observed, on the three pro-German projects on which Indian nationals worked in the United States, "the Germans were in command and the Ghadar men were treated as enthusiastic errand boys to be financed, advised, and ordered about. Ghadar party's participation in the [shipping of arms to India] project was nominal."[8]

In January of 1915 ten carloads of munitions arrived at San Diego by rail from Galveston under an original bill of lading of the Mallory Steamship Company vessel, SS *Nueces*. The most significant portion of the shipment consisted of 561 cases of rifles. These included 8,080 Springfield single-shot rifles of 45/70 caliber together and bayonets, plus 2,400 Springfield carbines of the same caliber (obsolete, with black powder ammunition), and 410 Hotchkiss repeating rifles of the same caliber, bought from the Winchester Repeating Arms Company. There were also 500 Colt revolvers of .45 caliber. The domestic value of these weapons was about $130,000. Ammunition for these weapons included 2,904,340 rounds of 45-70 caliber, and 100,000 rounds of .45 caliber, all of which had an estimated value of $160,000. The shipment was completed with 10 cases consisting of 5,000 cartridge belts, worth $10,000. The total weight of the shipment was 275 tons.[9]

These munitions were soon loaded aboard the *Larsen*, and a manifest for their shipment to Topolobampo on the Gulf of

California was prepared. Although there was considerable speculation that this shipment was destined for the forces of the Mexican revolution, both the Carranza and the Villa authorities notified the U.S. Marshal in San Diego that the arms were not intended for them.[10] Inasmuch as no embargo of weapons shipments to Mexico existed at that time, the shipment itself was not illegal under specific statutes, unless one took the broader view that these arms were destined for enemies of a nation with whom the United States was at peace.[11]

Considering that the primary intent of the expedition was to delivery the weapons somewhere else, the preparations made by the local agents in San Diego for the shipment to Topolobampo were thorough and elaborate. The real plan, engineered by the *Etappe* in San Francisco, called for the *Annie Larsen* to rendezvous with the 240-foot-long *Maverick* at the bleak, uninhabited Socorro Island, 800 miles west of the Mexican coast and 350 miles south of Magdalena Bay. At this point the arms and ammunition were to be transferred to the steamer and taken to Southeast Asia and ultimately to India, where German agents would assist native agitators in a revolution that would keep the British fully occupied.

The official consignor of the shipment to Topolobampo was a man named W. C. Hughes of New York City who had a business connection with the arms merchant Tauscher. The consignee in Topobobampo was one Juan Bernardo Bowen.[12] The latter individual became another of the several mystery people of the conspiracy. Federal agents later canvassed a number of residents of Sinaloa and adjacent areas of Mexico, and found no one who knew of such a person. He may simply not have existed. Eventually, a handwriting expert would testify that the signature of Juan Bernardo Bowen on correspondence was actually that of a man named Bernard Manning, a detective employed by the conspirators in San Diego at the time the *Annie Larsen* was being acquired.[13]

The rest of the paperwork for the voyage was soon completed. Shipping articles were signed, in which the voyage was described as from San Diego to "Mexico and return to any place in California, Oregon, or Washington, crew to handle all cargoes and to be discharged after the vessel is discharged and ready for sea."[14] This terminology reflected an announced intent of picking up a return cargo of railroad ties from the offshore Mexican islands, Tres Marias, which would be taken north.[15]

On the shipping articles P. H. Schluter, 27-year-old German-born naturalized citizen, was identified as the master. Lining up a crew had not been easy, inasmuch as word of the vessel's load of arms bound for revolution-torn Mexico had spread along the waterfront, and newspaper stories spoke openly about the mystery vessel and her cargo of weapons bound for Mexico. The crew that was finally assembled consisted of George Poppe, a native of Germany, citizen of the United States, serving as mate; and the following crewmen: Herman Gartman, a native of Germany, not a citizen; Oscar Kvalvik, native of Norway, not a citizen; Peter Olsen, native of Denmark, not a citizen; Frank Fukooka, an Hawaiian islander; Ed Smith, born at sea, a citizen; and John Seiter and Thomas Thorstensen, about whom no further information was reported.[16] Although the *Maverick* would later take a number of Indians in her crew as part of the run-running conspiracy, none was aboard the *Annie Larsen*.

In addition to the regular captain, a supercargo having full authority over the movements of the *Annie Larsen* was placed on board the schooner. This man, who claimed to be Walter H. Page of Kansas City, was actually Captain Herman Othmer, 39-year-old master of the 105-foot German schooner *Atlas* interned at San Francisco. While the *Annie Larsen* was still in port the charter party was assigned to Page/Othmer by Martinez, so this man in effect was to serve as both owner and master of the vessel. An American by birth, Othmer had lived in Germany between the ages of 9 and 15.[17] Another of the more colorful figures of the conspiracy cases, he was reportedly a resident of the Gilbert Islands, and had arrived in San Francisco in November on the *Atlas* after a 52-day passage from Jaluit in the German-controlled Marshall Islands.

Othmer's alias was an interesting choice of names by the Germans in that the United States Ambassador to Great Britain at that time was Walter H. Page. From the standpoint of trying to keep the people and events of this story straight, however, it was an unfortunate choice of an alias, since there was another Page, Arthur Page, who figured in the arrangements made between Hizar, Martinez, and Bowen in planning and implementing the voyage of the *Larsen*.

At least two passengers were known to have boarded the *Larsen* for her trip south. One was identified as T. R. or L. R. Palmer, an American businessman, who was apparently fleeing from business and alimony problems.[18] The other was a "self-styled Count Wilhem von Hardenburg" who is mentioned briefly in the reports of federal agents who later investigated the various transactions involved in the shipment of the weapons.[19] However, it is possible that this latter individual was one of the crew under another name since he was identified only as being aboard, not specifically as a passenger. Apparently, no one disclosed to the passenger(s) the real itinerary for the vessel.

The *Annie Larsen* cleared customs at San Diego on March 8, and departed for sea. In the declarations he made in clearing for Topolobampo the captain may not have had to perjure himself, in that the relevant section of Revised Statute 4200 required only that the captain swear that the manifest truly disclosed the port or country in which the cargo was intended to be landed, and did not require the captain to swear that he would land the cargo there. Furthermore, John B. Starr-Hunt, a young associate of Jebsen's, was scheduled to come to Socorro Island on the *Maverick*, and then to trade places with the supercargo on the sailing vessel, W. H. Page, after which as supercargo of the *Larsen* he was to keep that vessel on the Mexican coast for six months.[20] Thus, the Mexican connection was legitimate, and the vessel was officially committed to departing for that country with her cargo.

Upon departing San Diego the schooner was towed by the tug *Bahada* about 120 miles offshore, accompanied for part of the way by a launch with supporters of Pancho Villa in it. At a point about 100 miles south of San Clemente Island she cast off the towline and proceeded south. Within a day it was clear to all on board that she was not going to Topolobampo. On March 18 she arrived at Socorro Island and anchored at Braithwaite Bay to begin her long, and ultimately futile, wait for the *Maverick*.

The tanker, however, was running badly behind schedule. More than three weeks passed at Socorro with no word from the ship. The crew of the *Annie Larsen* spent considerable time searching for water on the arid island, and three wells were dug during this time without any success. According to the recollections of both the captain and supercargo, with her water and provisions nearly exhausted, the *Larsen* could wait no longer for the larger ship, and sailed on April 17 for the Mexican coast. Before departing Socorro, the supercargo left a note for the *Maverick* in a bottle tied to a buoy, with another copy given to the crew of a two masted schooner, the *Emma*, which had arrived at the island.

En route to the mainland, Othmer/Page offered each member of the crew $10 to say nothing to the Mexican officials regarding the cargo, an amount that was subsequently paid as promised.[21] After three days at sea the schooner reached the coast, and spent several days searching for water. Finally, the *Larsen* put into Acapulco on the afternoon of April 23rd, the same day that the *Maverick* was leaving San Pedro. At the Mexican port the authorities were immediately suspicious.

The USS *Yorktown*, along with several other American naval vessels, was lying at anchor in Acapulco. In the absence of the American consul who had been evacuated earlier because of the hostilities of the revolution, the senior naval officer in the area assumed the responsibilities of the consul. Although it is not clear that he was the senior officer present inasmuch as there was a cruiser in port, the commanding officer of the *Yorktown*, Commander Raymond D. Hasbrouck, assumed responsibility for dealing with the problems of the arms-running schooner. He recorded in his personal diary what happened next:

> Schooner *Annie Larsen* much speculated about in San Diego papers stood into harbor flying distress signals — boarded her and found out of water and provisions very low — gave her two breakers of water — would not anchor but stayed out and off entrance all night — looked queer — came in Tuesday morning, the 27th, and anchored — sent boarding officer and Captain Schluter came ashore to see me, his tale most interesting; left San Diego, March 8, with cargo of 13,000 Springfield Old Army-model rifles, caliber 45-70; nearly 4,000,000 rounds of ammunition, destination of cargo secret — under indefinite charter to parties unknown — under orders of supercargo, a W.

H. Page — have been at Socorro Island, Braithwaite Bay, since arriving there direct from San Diego awaiting steamer to transfer cargo. From indication arms are for Germans somewhere — suspect South Africa or the South Sea Islands or for a raiding party in some English or French colonial island or possession — filibustering expectation surely — supercargo I suspect is a German naval officer, has all the ear marks — decided German type.

Larsen held by Customs officials had got wind of her cargo — I went ashore and on my representation she was released. Two of her sailors deserted and again I went ashore and had my fat friend the Commandante round them up — drunk on mescal, quarrelsome — went off 5:00 p. m. the 27th and raised row on board — Captain hit one with belaying pin and drew gun — crew refused to get up anchor.

Annie Larsen sailed April 28 from Acapulco for Socorro Island to leave supplies for four marooned seamen. *Larsen* will seek a new rendezvous since her location is known.[22]

According to Peter Olsen of the crew of the *Larsen*, Commander Hasbrouck's account of the events at Acapulco did not tell the whole story. With the help of marines who boarded the schooner, the two troublesome crewmen, Kvalvik and Thorstensen, were put in chains overnight aboard the *Larsen* before they finally became submissive enough to agree to go back to work.[23]

Thorstensen charged in testimony at the subsequent trials that Hasbrouck not only had been responsible for ordering him into chains, but had failed to do anything about his complaint that the captain had refused to pay him any of his wages—other than his $10 hush money—and that the captain had struck him, which was a violation of the laws affecting seamen.[24] It is difficult, of course, to know what really happened in this situation and where the blame lies, but it does seem clear that Hasbrouck exerted considerable authority in supporting the captain of the ship in this instance, just as he had used his position with the local authorities to legitimize the ship's presence in port.

In dealing with these authorities, Hasbrouck's action in assisting the schooner to obtain her clearance from Acapulco raises several questions. He recalled later that he convinced the local authorities that the arms aboard were not intended for a Mexican port. If that were the case, the original clearance at San Diego had been obtained fraudulently, a federal crime. In his diary quoted above, Commander Hasbrouck expressed strong suspicions that the arms were going abroad for a military venture against the Allied powers. In that case, such a venture appeared to represent a military expedition against a country with which the United States was at peace, an act that was cited as a federal crime when the indictments were subsequently brought in 1916 and 1917 against the many defendants in this case.[25] Consequently, it seems that the Navy had an opportunity to have nipped the plot in the bud before it went any further, but did nothing to do so.

After leaving Acapulco, the *Annie Larsen* was unable to work her way against the prevailing winds from the northwest to reach Socorro, and eventually gave up her attempts to return to the island. She next tried instead to reach a second rendezvous island but was unable to do so. Crewman Peter Olsen later told a federal investigator that this island was at 172 degrees *east* longitude, which, if true, presents some interesting possibilities for speculation. Finally, with her supplies again running low, the *Larsen* started for home. At one point she was able to cadge additional provisions from a passing schooner bound for Sydney, but the trip up the coast generally resulted in short rations, as well as short tempers, for the crew.

This trip home for the *Annie Larsen*, with her cargo of contraband still intact, became a wandering odyssey up the coast of the United States while the German plotters in San Francisco tried to determine what their next move should be. Without a radio, she was unable to receive guidance from the *Etappe*. Although her sails made her independent of fueling stops, she was desperately short of food and water. Nevertheless, she deliberately avoided putting into San

Francisco. Ultimately, on July 1, 1915, two months out of Acapulco and almost four months after leaving San Diego, she arrived at Gray's Harbor, Washington. Here the local officials acted quickly to detain the ship, her crew, and her cargo.

Within a few days the German supercargo Page outwitted his guards by appearing in his underwear in the middle of the night in what was an apparent trip to the bathroom, picking up a stash of clothes, and going over the side into a waiting launch. In the launch was the German spy A. V. Kircheisen, known as K-17, who under the name Phillips had rented a car and driver for the escape. Page was hustled off to the waiting automobile and made his escape. He and Kircheisen spent the next ten days holed up in a cabin in the woods, emerging only to pick up newspapers full of accounts and speculation concerning the escape. Eventually, the two went east by train from Seattle, caught a ship on the East Coast, and worked their way as seamen back to Germany.[26]

Officials of the German government made a formal request that the weapons cargo which they had purchased should now be delivered to them. Early in the saga of the *Annie Larsen* and the *Maverick* the Germans had acknowledged publicly that they had indeed acquired these munitions with their funds, but they insisted through their ambassador in Washington, Count von Bernstorff, that the entire transaction was a legitimate effort to furnish arms to their own forces in East Africa, something that was quite proper under the Hague Convention.[27] However, after this admission was made to the State Department in the summer of 1915, von Bernstorff in October changed his tune, claiming that, with respect to the arms, "the German government did not make the shipment, and knows nothing of the details of how they were shipped."[28]

Inasmuch as the gun-running plot seemed to be reaching the point of resolution, the American authorities were not interested in turning the munitions over to the increasingly troublesome Germans who had changed their minds again and now wanted the weapons back. Eventually, the weapons and ammunition were sold at auction early in 1917, with an arms dealer, W. Stokes Kirk of Seattle and Philadelphia, acquiring the shipment for $9,650, plus payment of a federal claim of $1,173 and county taxes of $2,116, a small sum compared to the total of $300,000 which some newspaper stories had claimed the cargo was worth.[29] It is worth noting that Kirk was one of the suppliers from whom Captain Tauscher originally bought the weapons for shipment to San Diego. Kirk claimed that he would make the weapons available to states and to military organizations, but it would be interesting to know where they surfaced next.

Thus ended the first voyage of the German-Hindu Conspiracy, leaving unresolved the rest of the story, which the Tacoma *Tribune* called "the deepest mystery the broad Pacific has ever seen." From beginning to end, the voyage of the gun-running schooner had attracted the interest of the newspapers which filled their columns with stories that were replete with color and hyperbole. For the most part the accounts in the papers were relative accurate, but sometimes they were well wide of the mark, as in the case of a story in the New York *Herald* which reported:

> Four thousand Springfield rifles and 250,000 rounds of ammunition were taken from the filibustering schooner captured by the United States torpedo-boat destroyers *Farragut* and *Hopkins* in the Santa Barbara Channel, according to naval advices made public.

The story goes on to note that the munitions had been stashed in a secret location on Monterey Bay in California by Franz Bopp for shipment on the *Annie Larsen*, and that the captured arms and ammunition were subsequently taken to the Mare Island Navy Yard. This story was given further credibility by being published in a monthly wartime update in the prestigious Naval Institute *Proceedings* in 1917.[30] How such seemingly credible stories could develop at such variance with the known facts is difficult to understand.

Eventually, the owners of the *Annie Larsen* paid a $500 fine levied against her master, loaded her with Grays Harbor lumber, and put her back into the coastal trade. However, she now seemed destined for nothing but trouble. Within the next year she was involved in several near-disasters in storms off the northwest coast. In 1918 she went wandering again, and was lost on June 9 in a stranding on Malden Island, a coral atoll 1,700 miles south of Hawaii, while en route home from

Samoa.[31] After the captain had sent several men on a 600-mile small boat voyage to Fanning Island where they were able to send a cable message alerting authorities to the plight of the schooner, nineteen people, including women and children, were eventually rescued from the *Annie Larsen* by the steamer *Mastodon.*

Even though her role in the German-Hindu Conspiracy three years earlier had ended in utter failure, and her later years had been even more disastrous, the *Annie Larsen* still had preserved a bit more self respect in those final years than had her appropriately-named co-conspirator, the *Maverick,* whose adventures now deserve our attention.

CHAPTER NINE

THE GERMAN-HINDU CONSPIRACY: THE *MAVERICK*

The process of acquiring the *Maverick* and getting her ready to play her part in the German-Hindu Conspiracy was even more complex and time-consuming than that required for the *Annie Larsen*. The biggest single factor that complicated the process was the purchase of the ship. While the *Larsen* had been chartered, the conspirators bought the *Maverick*, an act that consumed considerable time and created a labyrinth of relationships and transactions. In fact, the ship changed hands twice early in 1915, with both transactions occurring *after* the *Annie Larsen* had left for Socorro Island. Still a third transfer would occur before the end of the year.

The 24-year-old ship had been built for the Standard Oil Company as one of the first built-for-the-purpose tankships. In 1906 Standard Oil of California acquired the ship and a large ocean-going barge from Standard of New York for about $250,000. Within the next few years the ship earned her keep carrying petroleum products up and down the west coast and to Hawaii. However, as tanker technology improved, the ship and her cargo systems had become obsolescent; consequently, Standard of California was not reluctant to part with her. J. C. Rohlfs of the oil company had indicated to a broker, Harry J. Hart, that the company was interested in selling the ship.[1]

From the voluminous trial testimony which was available later in a format that reflected "who visited and communicated with whom under what circumstances," it is possible to distill the essence of what seems to have happened in the acquisition of the ship by the Germans. Originally, von Schack and Jebsen had wanted to send the arms and ammunition to Topolobampo, and from there on another ship to the Far East.[2] Jebsen had indicated that one of his schooners could come north for the first leg of this shipment.[3] However, the two men then apparently decided that it was safer to use a vessel over which they had direct control for the trans-Pacific part of the venture, so inquiries were initiated about the availability of a suitable ship which they could acquire.

Joseph L. Bley of the Bunker Company, who had figured prominently in the *Olson & Mahony* case, notified A. A. Moran, manager of the Olson & Mahony firm and another principal in that case, that he was looking for a small steamer with a 100-

day steaming range, and suggested that Moran contact the ship broker Arthur Page and get an option on the *Maverick*.[4] Page had been alerted to the availability of the ship through his fellow broker Hart who had suggested that the two men jointly try to sell the ship, and split the commission.[5] The option was obtained, but the purchase price was too high, so Bley indicated that he would continue to work with Jebsen to locate another suitable ship.

As word circulated that a ship purchase was in the works, other interested parties began to move. J. F. Craig, who owned a shipyard in Long Beach as well as interests in several ships, apparently obtained from Page an authorization to deal directly with Standard Oil after the expiration of Bley's option. In the subsequent negotiations, Craig offered $40,000 for the ship with the company countering with a $50,000 price, or $45,000 if purchased through Page.[6] A sale agreement was concluded for the median figure.

Up to this point it had appeared that Craig was operating on his own, but now the German connection surfaced. Since the Standard Oil representative was reluctant to take a check for the amount of the sale, Craig visited the Bunker & Co. office where he picked up Bley, with the two men then visiting the attorney Hengstler who represented the German consulate. A bill of sale was drawn up at Hengstler's office and a bundle of cash was obtained, which was taken to the bank where a cashiers check was purchased and given to the Standard Oil representative.[7] On the same day the directors of the oil company adopted a resolution which apparently accepted the terms of the sale.[8] In this way, Craig became owner of the *Maverick*, at least nominally, on March 16, 1915. By this time, the *Annie Larsen*, acting in good faith, was already on her way to Socorro Island to rendezvous with the tanker.

Craig now had possession of the tanker at his shipyard where some repairs were being made, but apparently did not consider himself the true owner of the vessel. After collecting about $27,000 for those repairs, Craig declined to participate when he was offered an opportunity to be a stockholder in a corporation which would take over the *Maverick*.[9] The details of the creation of this corporation are even fuzzier than those surrounding Craig's acquisition of the ship.

Shortly after the initial acquisition of the ship by Craig, Fred Jebsen told the Los Angeles attorney Ray Howard that he had bought the *Maverick* and sold her for $85,000, and needed a corporation to hold title to the ship.[10] Howard subsequently put together the first corporate framework of the Maverick Steamship Company, and turned the ship over to this company on April 8, 1915. Newspaper accounts indicate that the directors and offices of the dummy corporation were not shipping men: B. W. Knoll, superintendent of the California Truck Company, who was president; John J. Eagan, a detective with the district attorney's office, who was vice president; and Howard, who served as secretary and treasurer.[11] The District Attorney's office reported, however, that these three men had been issued only one share each of blank stock, and that the bulk of the stock, 45,000 shares, was held by William Lutton, the janitor of Howard's office building.[12]

In July, 1915, Hengstler, the attorney for the consulate, made changes in the ownership of the company. Claiming that he had all the company's shares in his possession, he persuaded Howard to transfer the stock to another set of shareholders in the new corporation, three other men who also had not yet played any major role in the conspiracies. One was Leopold Michels, a well-to-do San Francisco importer who owned 450 shares, another was Harry J. Hart, the ship broker who owned two shares, and the third was George W. Hosmer, an employee of Michels, who owned a single share. Howard agreed to the change, but insisted that he be given a release holding him free of responsibility for any consequences.[13]

The change between the two sets of owners may have marked an evolution in the company's development. It is quite possible that Craig initially brought together Knoll, Eagan, and Howard, and gave them a bill of sale as an intermediate step in incorporating the vessel and in shifting ownership from himself to the Germans, after which Howard, lacking instructions from the absent Jebsen, set up the other three men as owners. There are several references in federal correspondence to the ship also being re-flagged from Mexican to American registry during her sale. Perhaps the original transaction established Maverick Steamship as a caretaker company which registered the ship in Mexico, after which the second set of owners gained American registration for the vessel. In any case, not only was the ownership of the *Maverick* highly confusing, but the source and amount of the money the second set of buyers put up, as well as who received it, was never disclosed. Since it was all German money, however, perhaps none had changed hands.

While the first set of "owners" was still aboard, the Maverick Steamship Company had been able to line up a charter for the initial voyage of its new ship. In the same way that the *Annie Larsen* had clouded her real intent via the cargo with which she cleared for Topolobampo, the *Maverick's* owners covered her intentions by obtaining a charter to take a partial cargo of oil to the Far East. This cargo of 10,000 barrels of oil was purchased from Standard Oil of California in April of 1915 for $6,744 by Harry J. Hart, soon to be a minor shareholder of the steamship company and soon, too, to emerge from nowhere to become a major player in the conspiracy.[14]

This oil was to be taken to Java under a charter by the American Asiatic Petroleum Company (which, by some accounts, was the company to which Craig had first sold the ship), signed by a W. H. Smith of that firm.[15] Agents of the federal government were later unable to find any record of the existence of either the man or the company, thus reinforcing their growing awareness that another giant hoax was in the works. Furthermore, taking a cargo of oil to southeast Asia where considerable oil was produced made no real sense.

In addition to the partial cargo of oil, other substantial weights were loaded into the ship, ostensibly as ballast. In the stern tanks a deck of boxes cemented together was created; these boxes were full of castings and tubing of brass and steel. Steel plates were also placed in the tanks; their anticipated use was not self-evident. However, one person who witnessed the loading, a business agent for a maritime union, ventured the opinion that they "could be used in the construction of small craft or submarines,"[16] an interesting speculation inasmuch as later reports from the Far East claimed that the ship did indeed have the makings of a submarine aboard.

As with the *Larsen*, it was not easy to get a crew together for the *Maverick's* upcoming voyage. The deck crew was a group of what were then called Kanakas; these men were Pacific Islanders, in this case from Jaluit, a German possession in the Marshall Islands. This group, however, was apparently not Captain Othmer's former crew of the *Atlas* which was later repatriated.[17] Although the local union halls were utilized to furnish cooks and firemen, and although extra financial inducements were offered by the company, many seamen wanted nothing do with the ship, particularly if they had gone aboard to check her out. Eventually, it was necessary to bring men down from San Francisco to fill out the crew.[18]

The master was a retired captain of Danish extraction named H. C. Nelson. From all accounts he was a man of poor health and an equally poor disposition, traits that would appear to disqualify him from the long and difficult trip which lay ahead. However, he had occasionally filled in as master for Jebsen on the *Mazatlan*, so his selection must have reflected his previous record and judgment rather than his present capabilities.[19]

The officers were the typical mixed lot found on small coastal steamers of that period. The chief mate was a naturalized Swede, the second mate a native-born American, and the third mate a naturalized Norwegian. The chief engineer was a native-born American, and his assistant engineers were naturalized natives of Ireland, Scotland, and Norway, respectively. Two of the engineers were replacements for men who had signed on earlier, but had decided not to make the trip.[20]

One other officer who did not make the original trip is worthy of note. Fred Jebsen had sent a captain named William J. P. Kessel down to serve as a mate, but he and Captain Nelson did not get along well. As Kessel explained later, "Captain Nelson was hard to get along with and refused to pay me all my money for expenses and wages, so I left the *Maverick* while he was still at Long Beach and came back to San Francisco."[21] What is significant about this relationship is that Kessel would wait in the wings, and later replace Nelson as captain of the ship.

Several other interesting people also were aboard. One was the supercargo, the previously mentioned John B. Starr-Hunt, a 22-year-old protege of Jebsen who had worked for the German shipowner for several years. Born in Texas into a prominent family, Starr-Hunt had grown up in Mexico, and was well educated in private schools in Mexico and in the United States. He did not yet enjoy the full confidence of his employer, however; he had been directed by Jebsen to trade places with the supercargo of the *Larsen* at Socorro Island rather than make the trip to the Far East, and then to keep the schooner on the Mexican coast for six months.[22] From this man, American authorities would eventually learn much of the story of the strange voyage of the *Maverick*.

Although the *Maverick* was shown in contemporary ship directories to have had a wireless set on board, the radio was physically removed from the steamer by her owners, prior to the trip. The *Annie Larsen* had no radio. Consequently, it is easy to understand why the two vessels were to have such a difficult time in establishing contact with each other and in effecting a rendezvous.

One unusual passenger was aboard in the person of a German sea captain who went under the name of B. Miller. Some reports indicate that he signed on as a storekeeper, but he does not appear on the official crew list. He was introduced aboard as a Swedish mining engineer who was going to La Paz to investigate some mineral property. He had been provided with letters of credit by Jebsen, and he was supposed to announce in San Jose del Cabo that he had paid 2500 pesos for his passage; he also reportedly had thirty or forty thousand dollars in gold with him.[23] His presence on board was apparently a ploy to legitimize the voyage, which otherwise looked a bit suspicious if the ship went to Mexico without a full cargo. He also had the responsibility of watching over the five passengers.

These five passengers were Indians, going with the *Maverick* to the Far East as an integral part of the German-Hindu Conspiracy. These men were carried on the crew list as waiters, with their country of origin and present citizenship listed as Persia. They were subsequently identified as being from Baluchistan, now in Pakistan, which was part of India at that time. They came aboard the ship without much personal baggage, but with a large number of heavily-loaded suitcases which contained tracts of inflammatory literature to be distributed to Indians.[24]

Elaborate instructions were issued to Nelson and Starr-Hunt for the upcoming voyage. The ship was to proceed to San Jose del Cabo at the tip of Baja, and from there obtain a clearance for Anjer, Java, via Pacific Islands. After leaving San Jose del Cabo she was to go to Socorro Island, there to meet the *Annie Larsen* and to receive from that vessel a cargo of arms and ammunition. The arms were to be immersed in the oil tanks while the ammunition was go into dry tanks which would be flooded only if necessary. The ship was then to proceed to the Sunda Straits, near Anjer, Java. En route she was to operate openly, and not attempt to avoid enemy ships. If she were stopped by a warship, she should not resist inspection. If she were inspected, the ammunition was to be flooded. If the hidden cargo was discovered, the bilges were to be opened and the vessel sunk. Under no circumstances was the cargo to fall into the hands of the enemy.

Upon arriving in Sunda Straits she was to be met by a small boat which would display flags from the international signal code representing an M over V, the same signal which the *Maverick* would be flying, or three white lanterns at night, after which she would follow the directions of the people in the boat. If she failed to effect this meeting, the ship was to go on to Bangkok, arriving there in the evening. There a German pilot would meet her, and the ship would follow his instructions. If this meeting failed to materialize, the ship would go on to Karachi on the eastern side of India where the Indians on board would take charge of the disposition of the weapons.

In the event that the expedition encountered difficulty, provisions were made for cable messages to San Francisco in a regular commercial code, modified slightly by the addition and subtraction of certain numbers. The general password for the enterprise was "King George," the only term that appeared in English in the entire set of instructions.[25]

The sailing orders for the ship, which were typed in German by Starr-Hunt, had been prepared jointly by Fred Jebsen and Walter Sauerbeck. Sauerbeck was an officer from the German cruiser *Geier* which had been interned in the fall of 1914 in Honolulu. He had been allowed to go to San Francisco where he had joined the staff of the *Etappe* at the request of its leader, Korvettenkapitän Wolfram von Knorr.

The *Maverick* cleared for San Jose del Cabo in mid-afternoon on April 23, 1915; her clearance indicated that she was in ballast, with only fuel oil in her tanks. On board she had provisions for a voyage of six months. Three days later she reached San Jose del Cabo, where Miller went ashore. Here the ship obtained clearance for her trans-Pacific voyage, a clearance which the conspirators had felt would be easier to obtain in Mexico than in the United States. After an overnight stop, she left on the 27th for Socorro Island.

On April 28, she arrived at the island to look for the *Annie Larsen*. The schooner, however, had left Socorro more than a week earlier, a fact which Captain Nelson soon learned through a first-hand source, several eye-witnesses. After the *Maverick* anchored, a small boat pulled alongside with two Americans in it. When they asked "Are you the people looking for the *Annie Larsen*?" and received an affirmative answer, they were brought aboard. In their possession was a short note from Page, supercargo on the *Larsen*, reading "This will be delivered to you by a member of the crew of the schooner *Emma* who will explain his own position. I have been waiting for you a month, and am now going to the Mexican west coast for supplies and water. I will return as soon as possible. Please await my return."[26]

The story told by the two men of the *Emma* was a remarkable one. They, and two Mexican Customs officials who were in camp ashore, had left San Jose del Cabo some time before on the small American schooner *Emma* with a cargo of bark for the port of Loreto on the Gulf of California. This small schooner had a notorious reputation as a difficult vessel to steer and control. To make matters worse, the captain, a man named Clark who had recently bought the vessel, had proved himself incompetent and the vessel had become lost. After sailing for many days, during which time the mate had died at sea, the *Emma* had eventually arrived at Socorro Island which the captain thought was a mainland point near Manzanillo. These four men found by the *Maverick* had declined to go any farther with the captain, and demanded to be left on the island where they had the chance of being picked up by a passing vessel; the captain had agreed, leaving the men on the island while he and the cook sailed on. When the *Emma* dropped the men off at Socorro Island, the *Annie Larsen* was also there, and the crew of the gun-running schooner provided the castaways with some empty water tanks, a few provisions, and a rifle. Since then, the four men had survived through rigging a primitive water distillation and recovery system, and using the plentiful wild goats for food.[27]

The *Maverick* took the men aboard, and provided food and shelter until the 6th of May. On that date the American naval collier *Nanshan* arrived, having heard of the plight of the men through the *Annie Larsen* at Acapulco. The captain of the collier, W. D. Prideaux, offered passage to the four castaways, all of whom quickly accepted. By this time Captain Nelson had told his own crew why they were at the island; now, he was inexplicably candid with Prideaux, announcing that he was waiting for the *Larsen* in order to transfer her cargo of arms and then proceed to Java. Prideaux found the ship's papers in order, and observed with reference to the captain that "He frankly stated that the only reason he had gone to San Jose del Cabo was because it was not possible to clear from a U. S. port for Socorro, but that he had no difficulty in clearing from a Mexican port for Anjer via Pacific Islands."[28]

Just as the further travels of the *Annie Larsen* might have been halted by the U. S. Navy at Acapulco, the further adventures of the *Maverick* might well have been interrupted by the Navy at Socorro Island. Inasmuch as subsequent prosecutions in the German-Hindu Conspiracy cases would charge defendants with violating a section of the federal criminal code prohibiting participating in a military venture against a country with which the United States was at peace, it is odd that the captain of the naval collier did nothing to prevent the *Maverick* from going ahead on her announced mission. Even though the tanker had no arms aboard at that point, that same circumstance would prevail later when a number of people were convicted of conspiring to violate this law through their actions in acquiring and outfitting the ship.

Late that same day the *Nanshan* left Socorro Island with the four castaways on board, reaching San Jose del Cabo two days later where the two customs officials were reunited with their once-grieving families. The two American seamen remained aboard until the ship reached San Diego on May 13, 1915, where they cleared quarantine and immigration.[29] Even the *Emma* managed to survive, arriving at Manzanillo where she was beached by the captain and his cook, thus ending quite satisfactorily the saga of the volunteer castaways.

After this episode of good will, it was back to reality for the crew of the *Maverick*. Inasmuch as Captain Prideaux of the *Nanshan* had indicated that the *Annie Larsen* had left Acapulco two days before he did and intended to returned to Socorro, Captain Nelson decided to remain for a while at the island. On

May 13, HMS *Kent* arrived; whether she was tipped off by the American Navy is not known. This cruiser, a veteran of the Battle of the Falkland Islands, sent two boarding officers who examined the ship's papers. Following this visit, the Indians aboard the *Maverick* became concerned about the seditious literature in their suitcases. After trying in vain to convince Captain Nelson that they should be allowed to bury it ashore, they agreed to burn it. Consequently, the thousands of tracts that they planned to distribute to their countrymen were burned aboard the ship that day at Socorro Island.[30]

On the following morning the boarding party from the *Kent* returned with several Marines to conduct an inspection of the ship. In a return visit aboard the cruiser, Captain Nelson was evasive in answers to the questions of the commanding officer, suggesting that his real purpose in being at the island, while somewhat secret, had to do with the "Mexican troubles."[31]

The *Kent* spent about forty hours overall in the anchorage. She was followed on May 20 by HMS *Rainbow*, a Canadian warship. This ship went through the same general process that her larger British counterpart had conducted earlier. The officers of the warship alluded to their knowledge of the tanker and her purser/supercargo Starr-Hunt whom they identified as a fellow Canadian, which, of course, he was not.[32]

After the departure of the cruisers, Captain Nelson waited for a few more days. Finally, after 29 days at the island the *Maverick* departed. Thinking that he might encounter the *Larsen* at another anchorage, Captain Nelson headed west, stopping briefly at Clarion Island for a few hours, and then on north to Guadalupe Island for an overnight stop on May 28. He explained to Starr-Hunt that he knew these islands well from his younger days when he worked as a sealer in this area. However, no sign of the sailing vessel was encountered at either island or along the way. On May 29 the tanker arrived at Los Coronados, a small island group in Mexican waters, just south of San Diego.[33]

There, the *Maverick* stayed for two and a half days while the captain and the chief engineer went ashore at San Diego, a seventeen-mile trip, in the gasoline powered launch which Nelson had brought along for such purposes. Starr-Hunt protested that as the supercargo he should go along, but he was left on board. From San Diego, Nelson called Jebsen's office in San Francisco, and discovered from the secretary who was closing up the office that the leader of the conspiracy intended to leave the country. While Nelson waited, the secretary, Sue Clark, called the German consulate and talked to von Schack. When the consul was assured by Miss Clark that she recognized the voice on the line from San Diego as that of Captain Nelson, von Schack told her to call Nelson back, and to instruct him to go to Hilo, Hawaii, where he would be contacted further.[34]

The chief engineer and the captain returned to the ship in the launch, bringing a few supplies with them. Thus, ended the first part of the *Maverick*'s search for her weapons cargo. After six weeks on the Mexican coast the ship had nothing to show for her efforts. On the afternoon of May 30, 1915, she was underway once more, this time for the "big island" of Hawaii.

CHAPTER TEN

THE *MAVERICK* AS A MYSTERY SHIP

By the time that the *Maverick* left the Coronados Islands en route to Hawaii, the once highly effective German *Etappe* in San Francisco had begun to come apart. Wolfram von Knorr, the former naval attaché from Tokyo who had directed the organization during its successes six months earlier, had attempted to return to Germany, but had been detained in New York when he tried to obtain a false passport from a dealer who turned out to be a federal agent. Fred Jebsen, whose resourcefulness and knowledge of shipping had been largely responsible for the imaginative schemes which had characterized the San Francisco operations, had dropped from sight, and would soon be on his way back to Germany. The German spy K-17, Kirchheisen, was facing the imminent loss of his job when his employer, the Pacific Mail Line, announced it would soon abandon its trans-Pacific service, forcing the courier to make plans to leave for Europe. Federal agents were putting together their lists of suspects, getting a lead on their locations, and making plans for the trials ahead.

The consul, Franz Bopp, had been able to get back to his post in the Bay Area in the spring of 1915 after his home leave in Germany. Bopp inherited all that was left of the *Etappe's* military support program: the star-crossed arms-running venture in which a tanker with oil but no weapons aboard was now headed west with only a limited chance of accomplishing anything.

On the afternoon of June 11, 1915, the *Maverick* arrived off the harbor of Hilo, the rainy sugar-loading port on the southeast coast of the island of Hawaii. Harbor officials had been given no information about the pending arrival of this ship; they now came out beyond the three-mile limit to find out what ship she was and what she was doing there. Inasmuch as the ship had not cleared quarantine, the boarding party did not come aboard until the following day. In the meantime, Captain Eelbo, representing the Honolulu *Etappe*, came out to the ship in a launch and handed up to Captain Nelson a note containing the essence of his orders for the next movement of the ship, a stop at Johnston Island. These orders, along with money to pay the crew, had been brought to Honolulu from San

Francisco as one of the last missions of the German agent K-17, Kirchheisen, the quartermaster on the SS *China*.

Heinrich Eelbo was one of two captains of German ships which had been interned in Hawaii as naval auxiliaries, inasmuch as they had been heavily involved in coaling the German cruisers on their voyage across the Pacific. His ship, the 7,490-ton *O. J. D. Ahlers*, was lying at Hilo; the other ship, the 1,735-ton *Holsatia* commanded by Captain Edwin Deinat, a reserve officer in the German Navy, was at Honolulu. During the time the *Maverick* was at anchor at Hilo, these two men would stay busy scurrying back and forth between Honolulu and the big island.[1]

On the day following her arrival at Hilo, the ship cleared quarantine, and the curious customs officials came aboard when she anchored in the harbor. Captain Nelson explained his voyage westward, but omitted the fact that he had tried to locate the *Annie Larsen* and to take aboard her cargo of arms. Somewhat suspicious, the customs officers searched the ship with the full cooperation of the captain, but found nothing out of the ordinary. After customs departed the ship, Nelson and Starr-Hunt went ashore to make the formal entry of the ship at the customs house. There, Captain Nelson indicated that his stop at Hilo was primarily to communicate with the ship's owners. He also announced to the officials and to the press that he intended to stop at Johnston Island to investigate the commercial possibilities of guano deposits there. After leaving the customs house, the captain and the purser visited the office of Hackfeld & Company, a German-owned trading company which also functioned as a steamship agency,[2] where they met H. R. Schroeder, a young German who had come down from Honolulu to meet the ship. Starr-Hunt referred to this man as the owner's representative, but American authorities later identified him more specifically as a former secretary to George Roedik, the German consul in Honolulu.[3]

Schroeder was unhappy that stories had already circulated in official channels and in newspapers concerning the mysterious ship *Maverick* and her captain's announced intention of stopping at Johnston Island en route to Java. He told Captain Nelson that the stop at Johnston Island was now out of the question, since the notoriety of the ship had precluded any chance of making such a stop undetected.

Left, the captain of the USS *Yorktown*, aware of the intent of the *Maverick*, could easily have prevented the mystery ship from carrying out her expedition to the Far East, but chose to do nothing.

Above, the *Maverick*, a cast-off tanker that had been acquired from the Standard Oil Company of California, became a mystery ship during an attempt to take a cargo of guns and ammunition to native revolutionaries in India. Right, the Army transport *Thomas* departed Manila at the same time as the *Maverick*, and encountered a dangerous typhoon north of the Philippines. Did the *Maverick* go down in the same storm?

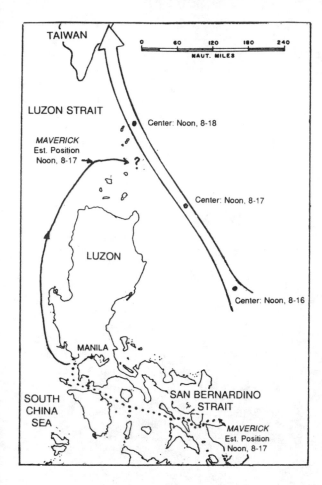

Leaving Manila, had the *Maverick* gone via Luzon Strait (solid line) she would have been caught in the center of a typhoon; had she used San Bernardino Strait (dotted line) she would have been well behind it.

Below, after the apparent loss of the *Maverick* in a typhoon in the Philippines, the American steamer *Maui* was one of three ships which reported being accosted by the mystery ship ten weeks later only 600 miles from San Francisco.

Schroeder indicated that he would go back to Honolulu, discuss the situation with the consul, and return with a new set of plans.

The ship spent eight or nine days at Hilo, during which time the crew enjoyed liberty for the first time since leaving San Pedro nearly two months earlier. Starr-Hunt allowed four crew members to be paid off, and hired three men as their replacements. Somewhat later, newspaper stories on the mainland reported several crew changes at Hilo that did not actually occur, such as Starr-Hunt returning to the United States to join Fred Jebsen, as reported by returning crewmen,[4] and Captain Nelson being replaced by another captain.[5] These erroneous reports of what was going on aboard the ship would continue indefinitely.

At the direction of Captain Eelbo, Starr-Hunt brought the ship's provisions up to a six-month supply through the acquisition of three separate orders of groceries from the firm of Hackfeld & Company. One set was for the crew of the *Maverick*, another for the five Indians aboard, and the third for the *Annie Larsen*. Apparently, the German planners still hoped that the cargo of arms could be delivered to the *Maverick* by the sailing vessel.

The special food for the Indians was a concession to the fact that they had become restless aboard. However, even this gesture could not change the reality that they were discontented with the trip. Several of them wanted to return to the United States, but apparently their leader, a man named Jehangir who signed his name as Hari Singh (neither name appeared on the crew list), was the keeper of five thousand dollars which belonged to the entire group, and would not dole out any of the money to individuals. Finally, a compromise was reached, in that the four men would go their own way but remain aboard along with Jehangir/Singh, and that Starr-Hunt would pacify the factions as best he could and provide spending money to the four men as they needed it.

The issue of Nelson's compromising the secrecy of the planned stop at Johnston Island continued to hang over the ship and her German planners ashore. Perhaps the dramatic highlight of the ship's visit to Hawaii occurred when a violent discussion was held on this subject with Captain Nelson, Schroeder, Deinat, Eelbo, and Starr-Hunt present. Deinat and

Nelson went at it aggressively, with the former maintaining that Nelson's public statement about Johnston Island was a stupid act, while the captain insisted that he had to be honest with the American authorities, and that he was not going to break the law for anyone. Finally, when tempers cooled, Deinat announced that no further attempt to rendezvous with the *Annie Larsen* would be made, and that the ship would indeed touch at Johnston Island as announced. The *Annie Larsen*, in turn, was to proceed to Topolobampo, an unrealistic expectation inasmuch as by this date the sailing vessel sans radio was well on her way north to Grays Harbor.

Eventually, with new crewmen and fresh provisions the *Maverick* was ready to depart Hilo. Captain Nelson was provided with cash in the amount of £2,000, the purpose of which, according to the receipt which he signed, was "... to be spent in India. In the meantime, said money is a kind of security in my hands against the good promises, made to me, and has to be given up at arrival at Batavia when outstanding claims are settled."[6] It was a strange agreement, apparently reflecting the Germans' continued expectation that the ship would get to India, but hedging that possibility by insisting on the return of the unspent money at Batavia.

On the *Maverick*'s final afternoon in port, Eelbo and Deinat came aboard with last-minute instructions. As Starr-Hunt recalled:

> In the afternoon Elbo (*sic*) and the Honolulu captain came aboard the *Maverick* and handed Nelson and myself each a letter. Both the letters were typewritten, one a copy of the other, and both addressed to the "Captain and Purser of the SS *Maverick*." The contents were merely what the Honolulu captain told us verbally at the meeting on the *Ahlers* as regards the future plans of the *Maverick*. The Honolulu captain then had a private talk with me alone in my cabin. After heartily cursing Nelson for his stupidity, he handed me a sealed packed which evidently contained a plate of something heavy. The letter was unaddressed. I was instructed to hand this over to Helfferich at

Behn Meyers upon arrival in Batavia. I did not
know then who this Helfferich was, nor did I
ask who he was. I was merely told that he was
the manager of Behn Meyers. I was asked to be
careful of that letter, and I was not to give it to
anybody else.   Shortly after, the Honolulu
captain [Deinat] and Elbo left, and we put to
sea.[7]

The *Maverick* departed Hilo on June 18. She was now an
established "mystery ship," but apparently no effort was made
by American authorities to shadow her, or to send anyone to
Johnston Island to watch her movements.   After a five-day
passage she arrived at the isolated American island ringed by
a coral reef, and found no *Annie Larsen* waiting for her in the
lagoon. Starr-Hunt and the mate, Oscar Erickson, went ashore
for a few hours to explore the half-square mile of land, during
which time they placed a dated message in a bottle, reading
"The American steamer *Maverick* entered and cleared here
today."

Aside from the fact that it represented the last possible
chance for the *Larsen* to make contact with the *Maverick*, which
was now a remote possibility considering that the sailing vessel
had been unable even to return to Socorro Island, it is difficult
to know why the Germans from the outset had planned that
the ship stop at Johnston Island. The German cruiser/gunboat
Geier had stopped at this island for several days the previous
September before coming into Honolulu to be interned, but to
suggest a relationship between these two visits—such as the
caching of weapons—would be pure speculation.

The *Maverick*'s visit to Johnston Island lasted only a few
hours. Upon her departure, the ship embarked upon the most
mysterious part of her westward voyage. According to shipping
notices, she arrived at Batavia on July 27, 39 days out of Hilo,
without, according to later statements of crew members, having
made any stops. The ship should have covered the distance,
roughly 6,000 miles, in 25 days at ten knots, the maximum
speed of the ship as reported by one crewman. Since merchant
ships normally steam at a speed within a half-knot or a knot of
their maximum speed, and since the *Maverick* was chronically
behind schedule, it seems reasonable that the ship would have

been operated at something close to her top operational speed. At nine knots she would have required 28 days and at eight knots the passage should have taken 31 days. Even allowing for the date lost in crossing the International Date Line, it is difficult to explain the extra week or ten days required in the crossing.

Later these time differences became important, in that there would be a number of allegations that the ship had stopped at various places during the crossing, carrying out her unique brand of mischief. Before exploring the balance of the voyage to the Far East, it will be useful to examine the question of the ship's timetable in reference to these rumors concerning what occurred during the voyage.

The reports published in shipping journals placed the arrival of the *Maverick* at Batavia on July 27, 1915. Recollections of the crew placed the date earlier; Starr-Hunt recalled the ship arriving at Anjer on the 20th where she stopped overnight before going on to Batavia, while the third assistant engineer, Carl Thorsen, put the date of arrival at Batavia as July 22. Both men noted that the ship passed close to Guam, but that she did not stop at any point between Johnston Island and Anjer. Even with these earlier dates of arrival, several days at sea were still unaccounted for.

The allegations that the *Maverick* had stopped along the way came from several directions. One of the federal officials who later investigated the case for the Department of Justice, Charles M. Storey, claimed that the ship stopped at Guam, the Marshall Islands, and the Philippines en route to Java.[8] As previously noted, Storey had an active imagination; he is remembered as the man who believed that the original intent of the conspiracy was for the *Maverick* to go to Topolobampo to push up river to San Blas with the arms for Pancho Villa which she had obtained from the *Annie Larsen*, although he admitted that no proof existed for his theories.[9]

Other allegations came out of newspaper stories reaching San Francisco in the spring of 1916 which reported that the *Maverick* had somehow acquired 5,000 rifles, and that this cargo had been jettisoned in the Dutch East Indies before the British cruiser *Cadmus* could place an inspection party on board.[10] This may have been the same incident reported in a Department of Justice intra-office memo from Storey to

Assistant Attorney General Warren: "[Special Agent Don S.] Rathbun says that M. J. Crago of Singapore told a newspaper man that the *Maverick* while in Batavia slipped out of the harbor one night and dropped part of her cargo overboard, because it was learned that the Dutch authorities were going to investigate her."[11]   Both these reports assumed that the *Maverick* had acquired a cargo en route to Java.

Other reports assumed that the ship dropped off, rather than picked up, a cargo along the way. Another reference to additional stops by the *Maverick* occurred later when the Special Agent in Charge, San Francisco, was examining the third assistant engineer of the ship, Carl Thorsen, producing this exchange:

> Q. Now there is a report that, "According to information the cargo of the steamer *Maverick* consisted of boxes with heavy contents, presumably fire arms, ammunition, and parts of submarines. These boxes are said to have been unloaded somewhere around the island of Mapia."
>
> A. We were never around there and didn't have any boxes of any description.
>
> Q. Another part of the report says, "It has been established that the *Maverick* called at the Marshall Islands, the Philippine Islands, and Honolulu where the Hindus are said to have come on board."   Where are the Marshall Islands?
>
> A. The Marshall Islands are south of the Hawaiian Islands, but we never went there.

The report which generated these rumors had been sent by the Chief of the Secret Service of the Police Commissioner at Batavia to the Dutch consul general at San Francisco in November, 1915. The relevant portions of that letter, from which American officials drew their conclusions, are as follows:

> According to information received here, the
> cargo of the SS *Maverick* consisted of boxes
> with heavy contents, presumably firearms,
> ammunition, and parts of submarines.
>
> These boxes are said to have been unloaded on
> the Mapia Islands, some 120 miles north of
> New Guinea.
>
> It has been established that the *Maverick* called
> at the Marshall Islands, the Philippines, and
> Honolulu, where the aforesaid five Persians
> seem to have come on board. They were
> claimed to own shares in the ship.[12]

According any credibility to this portion of the letter is made
difficult by other portions of the same report which seem
thoroughly in error. For example, the last line quoted above is
followed by this one: "In the vicinity of Galvestone (*sic*) part of
the cargo, viz. provisions, is said to have been transferred to a
sailing vessel, being destined for supplying unknown men of
war." Galveston, Texas, figured in this story only as the point
from which the original arms shipment was made by rail to San
Diego; furthermore, the transfer of the cargo of arms, not
provisions, was to have been from, rather than to, a sailing
vessel, and it had nothing to do with a man of war. This Dutch
official also thought that the Mapia island group belonged to
the United States.

As a result of the lack of direct evidence to the contrary, it
seems reasonable to conclude that the ship had arrived in
Batavia without having acquired or disposed of any cargo. As
with the well-known criteria for a criminal conviction, one can
establish *opportunity* in this case in that enough time was
available for deviations from the established course, and *motive*
in that such an attempt would be consistent with her owners'
commitment to stirring up trouble in behalf of the German
cause. However, mystery buffs and judges alike know that
there must be some real evidence linking the perpetrator to the
commission of the act. In the case of the *Maverick*, there was
only surmise, admittedly logical but nevertheless still
speculation.

Further evidence regarding the innocence of the ship is furnished by the fact that when she finally arrived at Anjer she was inspected by Dutch naval authorities who found nothing amiss; furthermore, this inspection took place before any of the possible opportunities for dumping any weapons arose. The arrival at Anjer occurred after dark, which is not the best timing a ship can effect when she is a stranger in a port. Immediately, the searchlight of a Dutch gunboat was trained upon her. A boarding officer soon arrived, but, after Captain Nelson pointed out that the ship had not cleared quarantine, departed after a cursory examination of the ship's papers. During the night three Dutch warships stood by. In the morning, a large group of officials came aboard to look over the ship and her papers. It was not a standard clearance procedure. As Starr-Hunt observed:

> Evidently, there were two Anjers, and we now discovered that we were in the wrong Anjer, although not very far from the Anjer that we wished to make. The Anjer we had struck happened to be a Dutch naval station. After examination we asked for and obtained permission to proceed to Batavia, and we set sail the same afternoon accompanied by a Dutch torpedo boat.[13]

Inevitably the question arises, why had the Germans decided to have the *Maverick* arrive at Anjer, rather than Batavia? Perhaps they felt that it would be easier to clear customs at a small outport, and then to proceed to Batavia. The original plan of exchanging signals upon arrival at Anjer, the flaghoist of the letters M over V in daytime or the three white lights at night, had certainly suggested the existence of German agents who would assist the ship upon her arrival, but with the nighttime arrival at the wrong anchorage, the ship was forced to improvise as best she could.

Shortly after the *Maverick* anchored at Batavia the next morning, a German named Kolbe who was the second mate of the merchant ship *Silesia* came aboard. After this officer spoke briefly with Captain Nelson, the three men, Nelson, Starr-Hunt, and Kolbe, went ashore. Following a visit to the American consul by Nelson, during which Kolbe told Starr-Hunt that he knew all about the adventures of the *Maverick*, the group motored to the residence of the Helfferich brothers, Emile and Theodore. There, Nelson held a long private discussion with the brothers, after which he and Kolbe left, leaving Starr-Hunt to carry on as Jebsen's official representative. The purser/supercargo then gave to Theodore Helfferich the weighted letter and other correspondence he had for him, including at least one message in cipher. Helfferich then noted that all the signals and passwords called for in the original plans had been used in keeping with his own understanding, and the code was also the same. At this point Emile Helfferich spoke up with some impatience, indicating that he had waited for the ship for three weeks in Sunda Strait. Once again, the *Maverick's* tardiness had been a problem.

The two brothers voiced their regrets that the plans had collapsed, because the arrangements in the Far East and in India were still in place and ready for implementation. As Starr-Hunt noted, with some chagrin: "Theodore Helfferich expressed his disgust at the *Maverick* being thrust upon him, and could not understand the object of her being sent to Batavia when she was not carrying the cargo and when she could have as easily returned to America."

A few days later the Helfferichs decoded the message that had been sent from Hilo. It said, in effect, abandon the project, salvage what you can, and sell or charter the ship if possible. The Batavia *Etappe* was authorized to terminate Nelson's employment as captain, and to pay off the crewmen and pay their return fare to the United States. At this point, the German-Hindu Conspiracy was dead in the water with respect to the delivery of any arms to India. Nevertheless, the *Maverick* would continue to be around for many more months during which time she would settle into her new life in Java as a ship whose notoriety had preceded her and whose custodians now despised her.

In the meantime, concurrent with the *Maverick's* passage through the southwest Pacific en route to Java, had been another last-ditch effort of the Germans to get arms to Indians or any other Asians who would resist the British. The 125-ton American-flag schooner *Henry S.*, registered in Manila, had been chartered by Albert H. Wehde for a trip to the Dutch East

Indies, and then on to Shanghai. Also on board was another German-American, George P. Boehm. Wehde had gone through Honolulu earlier where the captain of the interned German gunboat *Geier* recalled him as a German-American businessman from Chicago. Early in July of 1915 Behn Meyer & Co., the same firm that the Helfferichs were associated with in Batavia, requested permission to load aboard this sailing ship 164 crates destined for Shanghai from the German steamers *Suevia* and *Sachsen* which were interned in Manila Bay. Upon investigation, the authorities discovered that the shipment consisted of arms and ammunition. Not only was clearance denied to the vessel, but criminal charges were filed against the master of the *Suevia*, Herman Reichart, for placing certain navigational equipment aboard the schooner without the knowledge or consent of the insular customs officials.[14]

The munitions cargo in the *Henry S.* case presents further opportunity for interesting speculation. In the diary of Captain Carl Grasshof of the German gunboat *Geier*, American authorities found, along with a number of interesting references to the German espionage network, an allusion to 3,000 rifles which had been hidden by the Germans at Manila. These might have been the guns that were to be taken to Shanghai by the schooner, or, as an alternative scenario, it would have been possible for the *Maverick* to have stopped to acquire these guns, particularly in view of the fact that neutrality laws were not enforced rigorously in the Philippines. In either case, another futile German effort to create trouble for the British in the Far East had come to an end.

The resourceful British benefitted further by obtaining incriminating information from several people who knew about the gun-running projects, including Boehm from the *Henry S.*, Dr. Daus Dekker, a German agent with a Japanese passport, and Jodi Singh, from the *Maverick's* Indian crew. Even the German codes were revealed during the interrogation of these men.[15] As they learned more about the extent of the Ghadar movement, the British increasingly felt that the indifference of the United States to the violations of its neutrality laws was responsible for much of the covert activity.[16]

Weeks passed, soon turning into months, as the situation for the *Maverick* and her crew at Batavia began to stagnate. The Helfferichs explained to Starr-Hunt that it was becoming impossible to sell the ship because of the notoriety she had acquired and the pressure which the British were putting on the Dutch who had remained neutral in the war. Only a few people had even looked at the ship. As Carl Thorsen, the third assistant engineer, recalled:

> There was a man out there from the oil company who inspected the ship. He told us she was for sale and they wanted £20,000 for the ship. He offered £12,000 for the ship but the sale didn't go through. He was supposed to be a sort of inspector for some oil company out there.[17]

The Helfferichs tried to get officials of the Shanghai *Etappe* to take the ship off their hands and to find some use for her, but were told that Shanghai wanted nothing to do with the ship. In October, 1915, the Dutch interned the ship,[18] which made her disposition that much more difficult. Another interesting thing happened that month which would normally have affected her future, but in reality did not; she was sold again. The sale, however, was to an insider. Harry J. Hart, who had owned only two of the original 453 shares of the Maverick Steamship Company, now took over control of the company, although no details of the transaction seem to exist.

Little is known about Hart, whom newspapers subsequently described as the "prime mover" of the Maverick Steamship Company.[19] He claimed to have had 35 years experience in the shipping business, but he was not identified in any of the later reports of federal investigators who went to great lengths to establish the relationships and associations between and among the various defendants in the shipping conspiracy cases. Inasmuch as no German tie was conspicuous in his background, his motives should probably be regarded as purely financial.

The crewmen had been paid regularly during their time in Batavia with checks drawn on the International Banking Corporation, a bank in whose San Francisco office the German consulate maintained an account.[20] The Indians on board went on fighting among themselves, but Starr-Hunt managed to keep them from getting out of control by continuing to dole out money to them. Although it would be several months until the new ownership by Hart produced any change in the operation of the *Maverick*, the changeover apparently improved the situation for the crew. Those who wanted to come home were assured that they could soon do so.

Hart's first act that would have any impact on the ship's situation was the selection of a new captain to replace the unpopular and ineffective H. C. Nelson. In mid-November he chose William J. P. Kessel, the man who had worked briefly as a mate on the ship in San Pedro, but had quarreled with Captain Nelson. Kessel was a German-born naturalized citizen of the United States who owned a saloon in San Francisco patronized by Germans. Inasmuch as Kessel was known to be pro-German, his selection by Hart raises questions about whether the new owner was his own man or simply a continuing front for the Germans. Support for the latter theory was provided at the meeting held when Kessel signed his contract and was given his orders and code book. That meeting was attended by consul Bopp, vice consul von Schack, Capelle who had been involved in the cargo conspiracies, and Hengstler, the attorney for the consulate.

Hart provided the new captain with rather elaborate orders, calling for the ship to be readied to proceed to Tarakan, Borneo, to load a cargo of oil for Europe; the orders also authorized the captain to hire whatever additional officers and crew he needed in order to make this voyage. He was provided with $5,000 in cash and letters of credit, and was instructed to get back from Nelson the £2,000 which the former captain had been provided at Hilo.

One interesting clause in the instructions suggested that the Germans were still trying to effect some kind of clandestine shipment. In addition to the oil cargo, the ship was to load case goods in the t'ween decks. When Kessel asked von Schack whether that meant kerosene, the traditional case goods carried on tankers of that era, the vice consul told him that he would find out when he got there.[21]

While all this was going on in San Francisco, the crew was disbanding in Batavia. A group including the chief mate and second mate left for San Francisco, arriving in mid-December.[22] Two of the Indians left for Bangkok where they were subsequently arrested; one of these two would later become a witness when the German-Hindu Conspiracy trial took place in San Francisco. The other three Indians left for Manila at a later date. The Pacific Islanders drifted on to ports unknown. At the time that Starr-Hunt left the ship in late November, only the captain, chief engineer, third mate, and a German messboy remained aboard from the original crew.

The grossly inaccurate newspaper reports of the ship's adventures and personnel were to continue. On September 13, 1916, the San Francisco *Chronicle* reported the arrival home of a Captain J. M. Griswold of the *Maverick* who was quoted as saying that "I took command of the *Maverick* after she put into Batavia." He reported that there were no munitions on board, but she was to have taken some aboard and was to "have been used as a blind for some activities south of the Suez Canal."[23] While this man sounds real enough, there is no indication in any of the records that such a captain ever commanded the *Maverick*. Furthermore, correspondence from Hart to Kessel as master of the ship can be documented between November 20, 1915, when Kessel relieved Nelson, and September 20, 1916, when Kessel was reprimanded by Hart for inefficiency, a week after Captain Griswold reached San Francisco. Thus, one more mystery exists for the *Maverick*, the case of the supernumerary captain.

One interesting observation of this pseudo-captain bears further examination, his reference to "activities south of the Suez Canal." Recall that the German ambassador von Bernstorff had originally said that the *Annie Larsen* weapons were a legitimate German shipment destined for East Africa. Moreover, Starr-Hunt indicated in his "confession" that Captain Nelson had several charts hidden in the *Maverick*'s chart table which were of the Indian Ocean and which could be dangerous to the future of the mission if found by any inspecting officers from British ships. Starr-Hunt also recalled that a port in Africa, with a long name he could not remember (Dar es Salaam in German East Africa?), was a place to be visited or contacted according to the original instructions provided by Jebsen back in San Francisco. Thus, it seems quite possible that the Germans may have intended to deliver the arms to East Africa, either as a double-cross to the Indians or as a fallback alternative site in case things went wrong in making the delivery of Indian arms in Southeast Asia.

With Starr-Hunt's departure from the ship begins the least known and most disturbing part of the entire story, one in which newspaper accounts must be given additional credence because other records are so fragmentary. In his long statement which has otherwise provided many of the details of the *Maverick*'s entire story, the purser himself said relatively little about this period. Using the name of Rowan, Starr-Hunt left Batavia on the *Rembrandt* which was headed for Singapore, Hong Kong, Manila, and Yokohoma. At Singapore he was detained by the British who were aware of the *Maverick* caper and who apparently suspected the identity of the new arrival. Allowed to remain at large under a loose form of parole, the most stringent feature of which was a restriction on communicating except through a censor, Starr-Hunt indiscreetly wrote to the Helfferichs to get money and to implore them to keep the unpredictable Captain Nelson from coming to Singapore on his way home. This letter in early December, 1915, was smuggled out of Batavia by a Dutch citizen, but was intercepted by the British who now placed Starr-Hunt under arrest. Initially taken to the military fort, he was later put under a house arrest which permitted him to stay at a hotel, at the Raffles, no less, because of his American passport.

The first stateside word of Starr-Hunt's detainment came in lurid newspaper stories in March of 1916. The same story which had reported that the *Maverick* had changed captains in Hawaii, and that the ship had dumped her cargo of arms into the sea to avoid detection by the British, also spoke of the purser of the *Maverick* being jailed in Singapore after trying to get away from Batavia on a Dutch vessel.[24] In the fall of 1916 news stories in San Francisco reported that Singapore newspapers confirmed a recent International News Service (INS) story that four "Hindu" crewmen from the *Maverick* had been executed by a British firing squad in Singapore. Starr-Hunt, according to these reports, had escaped from Batavia and had gone to Singapore with the four "Hindus" to start a rebellion, and was still in jail there.[25]

Although confirmation of the fate of the Indians is difficult to establish, it does not seem possible that Starr-Hunt and these ex-waiters could have been in any sense working together on an uprising in Singapore at this point. In fact, two of the five Indian crewmen were known to have left the *Maverick* in the fall of 1915 to go to Siam where they were arrested; one of these men then told British authorities everything he knew of the arms plot. This man subsequently was a witness against the conspirators in the trials that took place in San Francisco at the end of 1917.[26]

Early in 1916 Starr-Hunt spent two months in the hospital in Singapore with an unidentified illness, during which time he received more than $3,000 from Maverick Steamship Company to pay his medical bills. After returning to health, in May over an eight-day period he dictated to the British authorities a long statement, often referred to as his confession, in which he described in great detail what he knew of the *Maverick* and her trip to Java. In December, 1916, with the acquiescence of American consular authorities, he was taken to England for further interrogation.

By this time, a new crew, identities unknown, had been placed aboard the *Maverick*. Captain Nelson departed Batavia early in 1916, and died a few weeks later while in Yokohama en route home in the company of Thorsen, the third assistant engineer. No authoritative reports have been located relative to the activities of the ship during the eighteen months between December, 1915, and May, 1917. One of the several poorly-researched books on the Ghadar movement written in India claims that the British cruiser *Cadmus* captured the ship and took her to Singapore,[27] but no evidence of this movement exists.

One clue to the ship's status, however, is the letter written by Harry J. Hart to Captain Kessel in September, 1916. It accuses the captain of failing to follow instructions by not requesting additional money to free the ship of massive debts incurred by Captain Nelson, of failing to take the ship on her charter to England, and of being "influenced by the German fleet (*sic*) at Batavia instead of consulting with the American consul."[28]

At about the same time, Hart was quoted in San Francisco papers as being ready to go to Washington to get the federal government to assist him in countering the blacklisting which the British were imposing on the *Maverick* in Batavia. Not only could the ship not be sold, he lamented, but if she were to leave the neutral Dutch port she would be seized by the British.

Hart complained that he had lost $300,000 because of these circumstances.[29]

It is interesting to note that at about the same time the German firm of Behn Meyer was using the courts to obtain writs against the American government for seizing German ships in the Philippines.[30] Thus, the Germans continued to use imagination and pressure against the neutral and unsophisticated Americans, even though they were forced to yield to the British in most matters.

In May, 1917, after the United States had entered the war, came the first authoritative news of the *Maverick* to be heard for some time. During that month the ship was acquired by the West India Sugar and Molasses Corporation of Baltimore. This firm, with the blessing and apparently the financial assistance of the United States government as well as the concurrence of British authorities, bought the ship from the Maverick Steamship Company, and installed as its marine superintendent and captain, George MacGoldrick.[31]

Captain MacGoldrick upon arrival in Batavia was distressed to find the ship stripped bare, with only the hull, boiler, and engine remaining. In addition, Captain Nelson and Captain Kessel had run up debts to Behn Meyer & Co. of 105,875 Dutch florin, or about $42,500, and a libel against the ship existed for this amount. This claim, which approached the price by which the ship had been purchased from Standard Oil three years earlier, was paid off by the sugar company in order to obtain the vessel free and clear. Further substantial payments were made to a repair firm which the British consul had authorized to bring the ship back into operating condition. Equipping and provisioning the ship was yet an additional expense and headache for the new owners. Captain MacGoldrick complained that getting the proper assistance in a German-dominated area was difficult, noting that "... what I had to put up with was awful." These difficulties prevailed in spite of the fact that Dutch authorities had provided day and night security guards on board the ship.[32]

Eventually, MacGoldrick was able to acquire a Dutch crew at Batavia, after paying bonuses and transportation costs. The *Maverick* sailed from Batavia on July 27, 1917, almost two years after arriving there. On the first of August she arrived at Tarakan in Borneo where the engineers reported that 16 leaking tubes in the port boiler needed further work. The ship was brought to Manila for the repairs, from which point the captain made his final report of the ship's situation to the local consul.

The *Maverick*'s departure from Manila marks the end of the recorded history of the ship, a history that has been reconstructed from newspaper accounts, documents of later court cases, and eye witnesses. Beyond that point, everything is a total mystery, as the ship apparently soon vanished from the face of the earth. The authoritative *Merchant Vessels of the United States* for 1917, in its list of ships lost during that year, indicates that the *Maverick* was lost after sailing from Manila on August 15 with 24 men on board; no other details were provided.[33] Other sources provide only a few additional details. Perhaps the best explanation appeared in the New York *Maritime Register* which on October 24, 1917, said in a story datelined San Francisco a week earlier:

> Steamer *Maverick* is out 62 days from Manila for Cienfuegos and shipping men are speculating as to her whereabouts. The steamer left Manila about the same time as the transport *Thomas* and the schooner *Irmgard*. Both the *Thomas* and *Irmgard* had to put into Keelung, Formosa, on account of being damaged by a typhoon.

Another report placed her departure from Java as August 15, and said that she was "posted missing" on February 6, 1918.[34] Still another account, this one in a San Francisco newspaper, reported that she vanished en route from Manila to the Panama Canal in August, 1917, to reappear later as a mystery ship of the eastern Pacific.[35]

She was indeed a full-fledged mystery ship at this point. What had happened to the *Maverick*? Had she become a victim of the typhoon? Tankers, particularly when loaded, generally ride well in heavy seas, and it would certainly seem reasonable to assume that the ship either had a cargo or had been ballasted with seawater inasmuch as she was starting on a long ocean passage in typhoon-prone weather.

A valuable clue to the fate of the *Maverick* may lie in the experience of the transport *Thomas*. This ship had left Manila on August 15, bound for San Francisco, with 2,000 American soldiers on board, apparently going by a great circle track. Two days later, according to her troop commander, Major General Charles J. Bailey, she ran into a typhoon with winds which eventually reached as high as 100 miles per hour. For four days the ship struggled through the typhoon, encountering the calm weather of the eye of the storm before entering the notorious "dangerous semi-circle" on the far side. Finally on the fifth day, after the weather had improved, the ship found herself in shoal water off what was described as "one of the little islands off the north coast of Formosa." The captain, recognizing the danger, had backed the engines, but the ship struck a rock before reaching deep water. Her bottom plates forward were buckled and torn, but the flooding was controllable. However, the ship was now too low on coal to make the Pacific crossing, so she put back toward Keelung, Formosa, for fuel.[36]

En route, she encountered the San Francisco-bound American schooner, *Irmgard*, which was dangerously close to foundering as a result of the storm. The *Thomas* then towed the schooner 180 miles to Keelung, after which the transport refueled and went on to Nagasaki to have her damage repaired before returning to the United States.[37]

If the *Maverick* had left Manila at the same time and on the same initial route as the *Thomas* she would have been somewhat south of the transport when she encountered the storm since she was making for the Panama Canal rather than San Francisco. Inasmuch as both the transport and the schooner actually survived the storm, it is difficult to understand how, barring some freak mishap, an ocean-going tanker would be capable of foundering under the same circumstances.

Furthermore, it is entirely possible that the *Maverick* did not take the same route as the *Thomas*. The Pilot Charts of the Pacific show the standard great circle route from the Philippines to the Panama Canal as making use of San Bernardino Strait at the south end of Luzon rather than Luzon Strait at the north. Had the *Maverick* gone this route, she would have been well behind the storm when she emerged from the strait, two days after leaving Manila, to begin her ocean passage.

The standard distance tables which have existed for many decades show the great circle distance from Manila to Panama via Luzon Strait as 9,347 miles, and 9,370 miles via San Bernardino Strait, or 23 miles farther going by way of the latter route. However, if navigators wish to break up the long passage (which would take 39 days for a 10-knot ship) and/or to refuel by stopping in Hawaii, which is roughly half way across and only a bit off the great circle track, the distance from Manila to Honolulu is actually 102 miles shorter by San Bernardino Strait than by Luzon Strait. Consequently, a case can be made for using either route.

Modern navigators taking advantage of counter currents in the Pacific might opt for a third possibility: a composite track from Manila to Panama, the so-called central route. This route departs significantly from the great circle track, but provides for faster speeds. These speeds can be achieved because ships not only do not have to buck the prevailing west-flowing winds and currents farther north, but actually pick up an east-flowing current of one half to one knot (which could increase the speed of a 10-knot ship by five to ten per cent). Joining this route via Luzon Strait makes the total distance to Panama about 90 miles farther than joining it by way of San Bernardino Strait. However, navigators of earlier times may not have had this hydrographic information available to them, so their choice of route was more likely to be made from distance tables or personal preference. Thus, it is impossible to know what Captain MacGoldrick had in mind when he was laying out his course as he prepared to depart Manila.

The tropical storm that had formed off Luzon was the second to strike the Philippines within a week. It was first tracked as a storm on the 16th of August when it was already off the northeast coast of Luzon (that date was by Greenwich Mean Time which would make it the 17th in the Philippines). By noon of the 17th, local time, it had become a typhoon and was headed straight north for Taiwan or Formosa. Moving relatively slowly at less than eight knots, it crossed the open ocean south of Taiwan on the 18th—which is when the *Thomas* would have received the full force of it—and hit the island that night, picking up speed as it went up the coast before blowing itself out in northern China on the 22nd.[38] The storm was indeed intense, but if the *Maverick* had gone by way of San Bernardino Strait she could easily have missed it entirely. However, had she gone by Luzon Strait she could have been very close to the center of the storm at midnight as the 18th of August, local time, began.

If one assumes, however, that because of the captain's choice of route or because of the seaworthiness of the vessel that the *Maverick* did not founder, what could have happened to her? What alternative scenarios exist? No German raider was operating in the area, although the *Wolf* was still capturing ships farther to the south in the Dutch East Indies. One possibility, albeit remote, is that the disappearance of the *Maverick* was staged. However, the captain and crew who had started home aboard the vessel do not seem to have been a part of the German-Hindu Conspiracy, nor were they men who had reason to engage in further mischief. Consequently, it seems very unlikely that the ship survived to turn up somewhere else, and no reported sightings at other ports suggest that she did.

Nevertheless, she did show up again, at least in perception if not in reality. According to accounts in San Francisco newspapers, the steamer *Paloona* of the Union Line of New Zealand, was westbound to Honolulu when her officers reported seeing the *Maverick* on the night of December 8, 1917, only about 600 miles from San Francisco. Attracted originally by signals of rockets and flares indicating that a ship was in distress, the *Paloona* changed course to investigate, soon discovering the distinctive features of the *Maverick* profiled against a background of ambient light. When the *Maverick* shone her searchlight on the liner, an act specifically prohibited by law, the captain of the *Paloona*, aware of the unsavory reputation of the small tanker, immediately put his ship back on her original course and left the area.[39]

The captain's reaction reflected the general feeling that the *Maverick* had become a raider. A San Francisco newspaper reported that "It is believed by many in marine circles that the *Maverick* . . . is lying in wait for some faster vessel which the crew hopes to capture and turn into a second *Seeadler*," the reference being to the famous and successful German raider commanded by Count Felix von Luckner which was active in the Pacific in 1917.[40] In fact, the *Paloona* had been en route to bring back from Tahitian waters the American prisoners taken by the *Seeadler* from the sailing vessels *A. B. Johnson, R. C. Slade,* and *Manila.*

Officers of two other well-known Pacific liners, the *Manoa* and the *Maui* of the Matson Line, also reported having seen the *Maverick* between Hawaii and the mainland at about the same time.[41] The one problem in all three sightings is that these Pacific liners had previously had little, if any, contact with the predominantly coastal *Maverick.* In fact, until World War One the *Paloona* had been a coastal vessel in Australia and New Zealand, and the *Maui* was built while the *Maverick* was still in Java. Consequently, the officers of the ships would not really have had a good basis for recognizing the smaller ship unless they had sailed extensively for other companies in west coast waters before joining Matson or the Union Line.

In any case, the *Maverick* had gone beyond being merely a mystery ship, and had now become a ghost ship. Newspaper headlines soon announced that the U. S. Navy at the request of the Department of Justice was conducting a search for the ship in the "South Seas." As one might expect, no trace of the ship was ever found.

To this day, there remains no satisfactory explanation of the fate of the *Maverick.* Although it is a disturbing thought to acknowledge that her captain and crew may have been unable to keep her afloat during the typhoon, that scenario comes closer to explaining her disappearance than does any other theory. Ships do sink with a troubling frequency in bad weather, despite the skills of shipbuilders and seamen.

As for the sightings several months later in the eastern Pacific, no one can be sure what these ships actually saw. Perhaps the *Maverick* had indeed survived the typhoon and had slowly made her way across the Pacific without any radio contact, only to seek help in a way that frightened the *Paloona* away, after which she sank. Or, perhaps another ship similar in appearance to the *Maverick* was experiencing some kind of difficulty which caused her to transmit signals which were mis-read by the New Zealander; the use of rockets and flares on a vessel has been an official distress signal for many decades, but the illegal use of the searchlight toward a potential rescuer may have created the specter of hostility. In any case, regardless of what theory one might accept in explaining the fate of the

Maverick, the reality remains that the ex-gunrunner definitely dropped out of the official registries such as *Lloyds* and the American Bureau of Shipping *Record* after 1917. Thus, the likelihood of her demise that year seems well established, even though the facts are not.

As part of the naval and maritime history of World War One, the disappearance of the *Maverick* counted for very little, which is perhaps why her story remains relatively unknown. But in the unique lore of the sea, few vessels have ever vanished under such peculiar circumstances. That headline writer in Tacoma who had coined the phrase "the deepest mystery the broad Pacific has ever seen" may not have been exaggerating.

Although the American authorities did not have possession of, or even knowledge of the fate of, either vessel in launching their case against the conspirators who had hoped to benefit from the *Annie Larsen* and the *Maverick*, they were able to move ahead. In 1917, as the cases against the earlier cargo conspirators were still being pursued, the federal government mounted the prosecution of the German-Hindu Conspiracy, with some of the same German and American defendants from the earlier cases appearing again in the dock along with the new group representing the cause of Indian independence.

The trials of 1917 and 1918 would be lengthy, costly, and spectacular. Like many such World War I prosecutions, the outcomes would satisfy public opinion, but would not make much difference in national security or the overall course of the war.

CHAPTER ELEVEN

THE PROSECUTION OF THE NEUTRALITY FRAUDS

For the federal authorities, putting together a case against those people who were now recognized as having defrauded the government was a new experience which was initially handled as timidly and awkwardly as had been the first determination of wrong doing.

Some of the slowness in starting the prosecutions was understandable; after all, the Department of Justice was now taking over an unfamiliar case whose nature had been largely a product of the decisions of the Department of State, Treasury Department, Department of Commerce, and Naval Intelligence, and there was much to be learned about the cases. Furthermore, interfacing with the British secret service which had done a substantial part of the investigative work on the German-Hindu Conspiracy presented other delays. Nevertheless, much of the slowness of the prosecutors was not easily explained, particularly inasmuch as virtually all the defendants had access to ships that could have taken them beyond the jurisdiction of the United States if they had so chosen.

In the summer of 1915 the first sets of indictments were obtained from a grand jury, numbers 5751 and 5752 on the calendar of the U. S. District Court, Northern California, District One. Many people involved in the cargo conspiracy cases surrounding the *Sacramento* and *Olson & Mahony* were named in these indictments. The first arrests of indicted individuals were made on July 9, only two days after the indictments were issued. These arrests were for people who were easy to locate and detain, largely shipping people in the San Francisco area. Other individuals, including those key Americans and Germans who had gone south on the *Sacramento*, were never served any of the legal papers.[1]

Inasmuch as the term has been used throughout this book, it may be useful at this point to sharpen the definition of what constitutes a conspiracy. The ordinary sense of that term, and perhaps the legal sense as well, implies secret meetings between several people in planning to achieve an illegal goal. It is not clear that, individually, the various events of this narrative—the coal shipments, the abortive *Olson & Mahony* scheme, and the *Annie Larsen-Maverick* venture—were truly conspiracies in this sense, inasmuch as the ambiguities of the neutrality laws made it difficult to determine what was illegal at the time. Perhaps, organized fraud is a better description of what took place in most instances. However, the German-Hindu Conspiracy has been described in a number of histories as a formal entity meeting all the criteria of that designation, and even worthy of capitalization.

Nevertheless, in addition to these specific intrigues, there appears to have been a larger conspiracy covering all of these episodes. Those who participated in the individual ventures were perhaps not conspirators in this larger sense, in that their activities were generally limited to only one of these major undertakings and/or were carried out purely for financial gain rather than out of sympathy for the German cause. But a small group of Germans and pro-Germans, most of whom were also profit-driven, figured in virtually every transaction and were in frequent contact with each other; these men have to be regarded as true conspirators. This group was made up of Joseph Bley, Robert Capelle, Fred Jebsen, Eckhardt von Schack, and Louis T. Hengstler.

In spite of the fact that many months had elapsed since the two freighters had acquired their cargoes and announced their intention of going to Chile, the Justice Department had not made adequate preparation for the prosecution of the case. These federal officials seemed as slow to grasp the importance of key elements of evidence as they had been to recognize that any laws had been violated. This was particularly true in allowing crewmen to scatter to all parts of the world before any statements could be taken from them. Complaining that he was unable to have his case ready during the tenure of the grand jury which had been convened and that he was working against the statute of limitations, John W. Preston, the U. S. Attorney, found it necessary to ask for a dismissal of the first set of indictments on February 14, 1916, and to start over.

The next two indictments, re-numbered 5866 and 5867, were issued against the same group of people on February 10, 1916. These indictments charged the defendants with violating section 37 of the Criminal Code of the United States, in being part of a conspiracy to defraud the United States by making false master's and shipper's manifests, thereby obtaining clearance of vessels not entitled to clearance from American ports. These defendants were clustered into several groups.

First were the four corporate defendants: C. D. Bunker & Company, the customs house brokerage firm owned by Bley and Bunker; Northern and Southern Steamship Company which owned the *Sacramento*; Swayne & Hoyt, the steamship company which owned most of the Northern and Southern Steamship Company; and Golden Gate Transport Company which had chartered the *Olson & Mahony.*

The largest group of defendants was made up of the individuals in the San Francisco shipping community who had become involved in the case. These individuals included the Rothschild brothers, John and Julius, who had sold the coal that the *Mazatlan* carried to Guaymas; Robert H. Swayne and John G. Hoyt of the steamship company bearing their name; the Flood brothers, George and James, who owned the Golden Gate Transport firm, along with Joseph E. Bien, their attorney who was a director of that firm; Philip R. Thayer, who had brokered the sale of the *Sacramento* for the buyers; Maurice A. Hall, who had carried the checks and cash around to the suppliers of the cargo for the *Olson & Mahony*; J. L. Bley and C. D. Bunker of the Bunker firm; Robert Capelle, the agent for the North German Lloyd Steamship Company; Frederick Williams, the unidentified buyer of the cargo of the *Olson & Mahony*; and a man named George Phillips, whose identify and role in the frauds were not made clear.[2]

Another large group of indicted individuals consisted of those Germans and Americans who went south on the *Mazatlan, Leipzig,* and *Sacramento* after the cargo fraud was perpetrated or were otherwise unavailable after the indictments were returned. These included Benno Klocke, the purser/supercargo who directed the movements of the *Sacramento*; Adolph Wimmel, the "supervising engineer," and Gustave Traub, the radio operator of that ship; T. A. Anderson and T. R. Johanson, captain and onetime mate, respectively, of the *Sacramento*; Simon Reimer, the *Leipzig*'s supply officer; and Frederich Jebsen, the German shipowner and naval reserve officer. Again, there was confusion about one of those names; the prosecutor Preston thought that Johanson was mate of the *Sacramento*, but Johanson had been replaced by Johnson before the ship sailed.[3]

SAN FRANCISCO CHRONICLE,

U.S. Grand Jury Indicts Consul Bopp
Official Is Accused of Conspiracy

Franz Bopp, German Consul-General at this port, and Eckhardt H. von Schack, German Vice-Consul, against whom Department of Justice officials at Washington and in this city state indictments, in connection with alleged violations of neutrality, have been voted by the Federal Grand Jury in this city.

Franz Bopp

Baron Von Schack

Charged With Sending Supplies to Kaiser's Warships and Violating Sherman Anti-Trust Law

(Continued From Page 1)

This account of the detention of the German consul and vice consul was typical of the extensive local newspaper coverage of the conspiracy trials in San Francisco in 1917-18.

Capt. Fred Jebsen

Who Is Reported to Be Alive and in China on Another Mission for the Kaiser

Crock, Car and Ax Fracture Three Skulls

Driver Argues With His

BOLD SAILOR JEBSEN SAID TO BE ALIVE

Story That He Is Working for the Kaiser in Orient Leaks Out

ALLIES ARE ON THE ALERT

Word Comes Mysteriously That Message From Captain Is on Way to S. F.

FRED JEBSEN alive! Captain Fred Jebsen, after many adventures, now in the Orient stirring up trouble for the allies as usual and promoting the cause of the Kaiser!

Fred Jebsen possibly now on his way across the Pacific to San Francisco to engage in some new and dangerous enterprise!

That is the story that leaks out of British and Japanese secret service channels to give new hope to his friends that one of the most picturesque figures on the seven seas is still alive and stirring, and to bear promise of more of those romantic tales of derring do of the plucky German who caused the allies so much trouble in the Pacific in the early months of the war.

Newspaper writers seemed as unwilling to accept the death of Fred Jebsen as did the prosecuting attorney in the case. Stories such as this one persisted, with the twin themes that Jebsen was too important to be used by the Germans as a junior officer in a submarine (which is where he reportedly died), and that he was too clever and too omnipotent to die.

Two German consular officers completed the list of defendants: E. H. von Schack, the vice consul in charge, and Henry W. E. Kaufmann, the chancellor of the consulate. Unlike embassy personnel, consular personnel do not enjoy immunity from the laws of the country in which they represent their own government; consequently, the German consulate in San Francisco, along with the one in Honolulu, would surrender several of its staff to American authorities before all the cases were concluded.

An explanation of the relationship of the various legal cases, while a bit confusing, is necessary to show the overlap between these cases. Correspondence among the United States attorneys suggests that as the several cases grew, there was an attempt to consolidate and refine the charges against various defendants. For example, a final case against the *Sacramento-Olson & Mahony* defendants, number 6131, seems to have served to consolidate or repeat the charges made under the indictments in cases 5866 and 5867.

In terms of duplication or overlap, it seems clear that there were additional convictions in the 6131 case against all those convicted in cases 5866-67. The *Sacramento* case also introduced charges against a few people whose role was apparently limited to the Hindu conspiracies, although the charges against this group of people were generally disposed of through other cases. One additional defendant was picked up in the 6131 case who was not included in the earlier cases: Louis T. Hengstler, attorney for the German consulate. His non-indictment in the earlier case was perhaps an erroneous oversight inasmuch as he had been instrumental in setting up the peculiar escrow arrangement whereby the *Alexandria* was to revert to her German owners when it became advantageous to do so.

Most of the shipping people and German diplomats who were a part of the Hindu Conspiracy, some of whom had also been indicted or pled guilty in cases 5866-67, were also indicted in a huge case numbered 6133 which was known for legal purposes as U. S. v. RAM CHANDRA et al. This case became the *cause celebre* of the west coast shipping scandals of the war years. In addition to the *Maverick-Annie Larsen* adventure, this case dealt with a number of acts of espionage by various defendants including a number of resident aliens from India.

After sorting out the somewhat less complex cargo conspiracies, we can turn to this larger and more complicated case.

The prosecution of the cargo conspiracy cases was directed by the U. S. Attorney in San Francisco, John W. Preston, supported by the assistant attorney, Mrs. Annette Adams. Although the cases were prosecutions under the federal criminal code, the violations were all what would be today called "white collar" crimes; consequently, federal attorneys enjoyed considerable latitude in plea bargaining and deal making. The goal of the Justice Department seems to have been to prosecute the most flagrantly and arrogantly guilty ones, to grant immunity to those who would testify against others, to go easy when the age and/or state of health of the defendant was such that he might not have the stamina to endure imprisonment, and to extract guilty pleas leading to fines in lieu of prison time to the greatest extent possible.

As he planned his strategy, prosecutor Preston conveyed to his superiors how he felt about various defendants. For example, he believed that grounds existed for a light sentence for Swayne in cases 5866-67, pointing out that this man had taken full responsibility for the acts of the Northern and Southern Steamship Company and had absolved Thayer and Hoyt from any responsibility. Preston considered Thayer egotistical, but felt that this man had been largely unaware of what was going on; similarly, Hoyt was regarded as a silent partner who did not participate actively in the daily operations of the steamship company.

Another reason cited by Preston for leniency for Swayne was the fact that the shipping official, although fully involved in the *Sacramento* affair, had subsequently played a significant role in preventing further use of American vessels in supplying coal to the German fleet. On a trip to New York, Swayne had learned that the American-flag *Minnesotan* was clearing from Newport News to Cape Horn, and had made inquiries which led him to believe that the ship's cargo of coal was intended for the German fleet. He communicated his suspicion to a British subject who was an official of the Canadian Bank of Commerce; this man notified a British consul who in turn informed the British Admiralty. This information was partly responsible for the British decision to dispatch the cruiser squadron under Admiral Sturdee which defeated the Germans at the Falkland

Islands. The British, said Preston, were convinced of the importance of the information provided by Swayne and thought that he should not be punished at all. Preston, however, was not so willing to forgive,[4] and his position on this shipping official changed from time to time.

With respect to other defendants, Preston observed that the Flood brothers were "of a shady reputation" in business, and knew that they were helping the Germans; however, the fact that they had withdrawn their request for clearance for the *Olson & Mahony* was extenuating. Bunker was old and incurably ill, and should be let off lightly; the same was true of Henry Kaufmann of the German consulate.

Several noble and self-sacrificing gestures were made by defendants in accepting responsibility for criminal behavior, but these actions may have been attempts to earn sympathy and tolerance for the individuals who made such gestures. The example of Swayne absolving his partners Hoyt and Thayer from blame in the creation of the Northern and Southern Steamship Company has already been cited. In addition, Franz Bopp and E. H. von Schack asked that clemency be shown in the case of Kaufmann, Sauerbeck, Capelle, Hart, Hengstler, Captains Deinat and Eelbo, and Bley; of this group von Schack said, "These men are all innocent and I am telling the absolute truth as I hope eventually to go to heaven, or to hell if it be perjury."[5] Similarly, J. L. Bley told the U. S. Attorney that he was prepared to be indicted, if by so doing he could prevent the indictment of other persons "higher up," an action which might "involve the two countries."[6]

Among the corporate defendants, the first round of the cargo conspiracy cases eventually produced guilty findings against Bunker & Co., Northern and Southern Steamship Company, and Golden Gate Transport Company. A nolle prosequi declaration was made in the case of the Swayne & Hoyt Co., largely because the federal authorities expected later to be able to come down heavily on Robert H. Swayne individually in extracting financial restitution. It is not clear whether these cases were actually tried separately, or were merged into the later and larger case, number 6131.

Only six individuals were found guilty in the first cases, 5866 and 5867. These people were Henry W. E. Kaufmann of the German consulate, and from the shipping world, J. L. Bley,

C. D. Bunker, Robert H. Swayne, Robert Capelle, and T. A. Anderson. Nolle prosequi determinations were made for Maurice A. Hall, the Rothschild brothers, Philip R. Thayer, John G. Hoyt, the Flood brothers, and Joseph Bien. The same six people were also found guilty in case 6131, generally known as the *Sacramento* Neutrality Case, together with Louis T. Hengstler who was not a part of the earlier indictments. Curiously, a number of key figures from the German-Hindu Conspiracy were also nolle prosequied in case 6131, most of whom were ultimately found guilty in case 6133, U. S. v. RAM CHANDRA et al.

It was also odd that the name of von Schack, the vice consul, did not appear on a list of those found guilty in any of the earlier cases, although in discussing him prior to the prosecution of the main case in the German Hindu Conspiracy the federal attorneys referred to his three earlier convictions. These earlier convictions were in other cases concerning the Germans, particularly those involving sabotage and explosions in the Pacific Northwest and Canada which were carried out by hired Americans or by zealous Hindus. In these cases Franz Bopp was the lead defendant; he had not been included in the prosecution of the earlier cargo cases because he had not been in the United States at the time of these conspiracies.

The most interesting name which was missing from the list of defendants in all the cases was that of John B. Starr-Hunt. This man had an intimate knowledge of Fred Jebsen's operations, the events surrounding the voyage of the *Maverick*, and the intentions of the Germans. This background was so valuable that the young man was offered immunity from prosecution if he testified against the conspirators, which he willingly agreed to do. He was even allowed subsequently to enlist in the U. S. Army as a demonstration of his allegiance to the United States.

For reasons known only to the prosecution, case 6133 was tried prior to 6131, even though the events that were a part of the Hindu case had occurred after those of the cargo conspiracies. Perhaps the prosecutors felt that this was the key case that would convict the largest number of people, leaving the other cases to be mopped up later at the convenience of the government. Perhaps, too, the prosecutors did not want to lose momentum; in the fall of 1917, Americans, including those serving on juries, had become impatient with German duplicity—even that which had been carried out while the United States was neutral—and to have waited until 1918 to bring these cases to trial would have run the risk of the war ending before these cases could be tried.

The trial of the German-Hindu Conspiracy case, to say the least, brought color, intrigue, conflict, and many other unusual dimensions into the courtroom in San Francisco against nearly one hundred defendants. As one contemporary historian described the scene, "Their trial was one of the most cumbersome and interesting cases ever heard in an American court. It began on November 19, 1917, in San Francisco, with Judge Van Fleet on the bench. Witness after witness recited his story of adventure, each stranger than the last, and all stranger than fiction."[7]

Another contemporary observer was even more eloquent. The British secret service agent Henry Landau noted:

> The trial of these men was one of the most picturesque ever conducted in an American court. The turbaned Hindus lent an Oriental atmosphere. Among the evidence were publications in six Indian dialects, also coded messages, all of which called for constant translation by interpreters and cryptographers. Witness after witness recited his amazing story of adventure. The action shifted quickly between the three focal points, Berlin, the United States, and India, with intermediate scenes laid in Japan, China, Afghanistan, and the South Seas.[8]

The principal prosecutors were again Preston and Mrs. Adams. By this time, Preston had been named special assistant for war work to the Attorney General of the United States, but he returned to San Francisco to conduct the prosecution because of his familiarity with the various cases. A number of attorneys represented the large number of defendants. The German consular employees were represented by Theodore J. Roche, a prominent local attorney who was also a police commissioner for the City of San Francisco. His law firm, Sullivan, Roche, and Sullivan, withdrew from the case in December, but Roche himself remained as the leader of the legal team which also included his partners, the Sullivans, in defense of most of the consular officers as well as Bley and Capelle. Representing Wilhelm von Brincken and some of the Hindus was George A. McGowan; although no comment to this effect was made in the press, this man was apparently von Brincken's former father-in-law. Representing the balance of the Hindus were Charles Sferlazzo, Timothy Healy, and Robert M. Royce. German merchant captains Deinat and Eelbo were represented by A. P. Black while Bert Schlesinger and Otto Irvine Wise represented the San Francisco businessmen Michels and Hart. Maurice Hall's lawyer was Edgar Peixotta.

Unfortunately, as a result of a courthouse fire which destroyed the original copy in the United States, no full transcript of this monumental trial seems to exist within reasonable access of American researchers. One writer dealing with the German-Hindu Conspiracy found it necessary to travel to London to review a 75-volume set of the transcript at the India Office Library.[9] In the absence of the transcript, staff correspondence within the Department of Justice and newspaper accounts provide the bulk of what we know today of this trial.

The local newspapers covered the trial with daily summaries of one or two columns, but papers outside of the Bay Area did not give it the broad coverage that such an important case would presumably mandate. Perhaps by late 1917 there was simply so much war news that a trial for earlier neutrality violations did not seem to have the same news value that a battle or a sinking of a ship might have.

For months the trial went on, occupying more than 80 days of court sessions. Witness after witness testified as to the nature and extent of the German-Hindu Conspiracy. The founding of the Ghadar movement including its strong roots in the Bay Area, the travels of its members all over the world, the recognition by the German government of the movement's potential value against the British, German funding and guidance for various kinds of espionage including the ill-fated *Annie Larsen-Maverick* venture—all these events were covered in great detail.

During the trial, another strange chapter was played out in the overall story of German supporters within the west coast maritime community who were trying to assist the Kaiser. In March, 1918, with apparently no direct connection to the San Francisco conspiracies, the American schooner *Alexander Agassiz* enjoyed a moment of notoriety when she was captured by the U. S. Navy off Mazatlan while engaged in an abortive effort by a comic-opera group to operate a German surface raider in Mexican waters. With this incident, German efforts to use west coast ships to aid their cause had come full circle since the days of the *Mazatlan*; in the words of the classic but nonetheless relevant cliché, these efforts had gone from the sublime to the ridiculous. When the schooner subsequently was taken to Los Angeles and subjected to a prize court hearing, this legal action momentarily occupied some of the personnel of the Department of Justice from the San Francisco cases who were utilized in the prosecution of the raider crew. Several German seamen were convicted for their role in this action, but no American of any consequence was involved, making it possible to dispose of the case quickly and to continue with the more important cases farther north.[10]

Back in San Francisco, little in the way of startling revelations emerged from the ongoing trial, but a few interesting flare-ups occurred, reflecting the tensions among the defendants. One such incident took place early in the trial when Dr. C. K. Chakravarty, the leader appointed in Berlin to lead the Hindu Conspiracy in the United States, admitted to the truth of some damaging evidence introduced by a detective of the New York City Police Department. Franz Bopp, the German consul, sprang from his feet, fists clenched, and shouted at the witness, "You are spoiling the whole case!"

Considerable animosity had developed between the Germans and Chakravarty. The Hindu leader had apparently been given hundreds of thousands of dollars by the German government to carry out the work of the conspiracy, but had siphoned off $60,000 for his own real estate investments. Toward the end of the trial, Bopp and Chakravarty became involved in another exchange which was picked up by reporters. To Bopp's question, "You say you were inspired by patriotism?," Chakravarty replied, "Yes." Bopp then responded, "Patriotism and $60,000."[11]

Infighting among the Indians became widespread during the trial. Some of this divisiveness may have reflected the religious differences between Hindus, Sikhs, and Moslems, but other unhappiness surfaced as various leaders such as Chakravarty and Ram Chandra were shown to have spent large amounts of money entrusted to them which did not go to further the cause of any rebellion or independence movement. Hayardan Das, one of the five Indians who had gone out to the Orient aboard the *Maverick*, testified that he had been "sold" to the Germans by Ram Chandra for $2,000 when he was sent aboard the ship. Das observed that the rules of the group provided that anyone who exposed secrets or grafted money must be killed, and that "Ram Chandra himself is the biggest grafter in the crowd."[12]

Animosity among defendants also surfaced within the more tightly-knit German group. Wilhelm von Brincken, the military attaché who was connected largely with the sabotage activities carried out by the consulate, angered Bopp and von Schack when he entered a plea of guilty early in the trial, along with some of the lesser figures of the German group. Bopp and von Schack, who had already been serving time in prison for their role in the sabotage cases, took the position that their duty to Germany precluded any use of a guilty plea, even to save themselves further prosecution and imprisonment.

In an effort to show support for their cause, attorneys for some of the Hindu defendants introduced into evidence the recent pacifist writings of William Jennings Bryan who had been Secretary of State in the Wilson cabinet until his resignation in 1915 when he was replaced by Robert Lansing. Bryan was subpoenaed by the defense, but did not come to San Francisco.

The most dramatic moment of the trial occurred on its final day, Tuesday, April 23, 1918. Judge Van Fleet had begun his charge to the jury by saying:

> This is a free country, and we do not question the right of any man within our borders, whatever his race, nationality, or allegiance, to entertain opinions and convictions . . . so long as those convictions are not given voice or acted upon in a way to transgress our laws or jeopardize the safety of our country.

What the defendants, be they Hindu, German,
or American, are here to answer for are acts
alleged to have been wantonly committed by
them which contravene the statutes of this
country, enacted for its peace and safety and to
protect it against the danger of international
complications and difficulties with its neighbors
with whom it is at peace through the violation
of its laws governing our neutrality.

As he finished his instructions, the judge and jury retired to
their respective chambers, leaving the attorneys to collect their
papers as the session came to an end. One of the turbaned
Hindus, Ram Singh, who had previously been one of the quieter
defendants, walked across the courtroom to Ram Chandra,
pulled out an automatic pistol, and at close range fired three
shots into Chandra's body. As the victim fell to the floor,
attorney Stanley Moore wrestled Ram Singh away while the
Hindu continued firing. During a moment when the two
struggling men were apart, U. S. Marshal James B. Holohan
shot the assailant, killing him instantly. When Singh slumped
to the floor, one hand was locked in a death grip around a shoe
of assistant U. S. Attorney Annette Adams.

It is not clear whether the jury learned of what had
happened in the courtroom in the morning, but they wasted no
time in bringing in their verdict the evening of the same day.
Of all the defendants, only John Craig, the Long Beach
shipbuilder, was found not guilty; the others were all found
guilty as charged.

On April 30, 1918, the sentences for the convicted
defendants in case 6133 were pronounced by Judge Van
Fleet.[13] The sentences varied considerably, with only the two
harshest sentences being the same, those going to Franz Bopp
and E. H. von Schack who each received a $10,000 fine and
two years in prison, the maximum sentenced allowed by law.
Wilhelm von Brincken was sentenced to two years in prison,
but was not fined, apparently in response to his plea of guilty.
Of the other Germans, Lieutenant Walter Sauerbeck from the
Geier was fined $2,000 and sentenced to one year in prison;
Captain Deinat was fined $1,500 and sentenced to 10 months
in jail, while his counterpart Captain Eelbo inexplicably was

fined only $1,000 and sent to jail for six months; and Charles Lattendorf, von Brincken's secretary, received a sentence of one year in jail.

Prior to the completion of the trial, those Germans who had pled guilty during the course of the trial had already been sentenced. Roedik and Schroeder from the consulate in Honolulu had been fined $10,000 and $5,000 respectively, and Kaufmann from the San Francisco consulate was fined $5,000 or 6 months in jail. Apparently no further confinement was prescribed by these sentences.

Among the American shipping men, Robert Capelle was sentenced to 15 months in prison and a $7,500 fine, Joseph Bley to 15 months in prison and a $5,000 fine, Harry Hart to 6 months in jail and a $5,000 fine, J. Clyde Hizar to one year in prison and a $5,000 fine, Louis T. Hengstler to a $5,000 fine and four months in jail (the confinement portion being immediately canceled, the result of a stirring denunciation of Germany which Hengstler made in court),[14] Bernard Manning to 9 months in jail and a $1,000 fine, and Moritz Stack von Goldzheim to 6 months in jail and a $1,000 fine. The role of this final defendant, who was described as a real estate and insurance broker, in the German-Hindu Conspiracy was virtually undetectable, but apparently he and Capelle were engaged in some joint business ventures.[15] His only overt act as a conspirator seems to have been in enlisting the services of his niece in German to forward letters for Har Dayal and other persons in Europe.[16]

Thirteen of the Hindus received sentences, ranging from 22 months in prison for Taraknath Das, an author and lecturer, through 60 days in jail and a $5,000 fine for Dr. Chakravarty, down to only 60 days in jail for lesser defendants such as undergraduate students. It is difficult to assess the fairness of these sentences because so little information was reported by the press on the activities of these individuals.

It is somewhat easier to evaluate the sentences awarded to the Caucasian defendants. For the most part the sentences for these defendants in all the trials seemed commensurate with the degree of guilt. A few conspicuous exceptions existed, however, including Captain Eelbo receiving a lighter sentence than Captain Deinat, von Goldzheim receiving any sentence at all, and Hengstler talking his way out of prison by repudiating his homeland.

Later in 1918 the *Sacramento* case, 6131, was tried as the mopping-up of the larger case. On December 23, the court pronounced judgment upon seven of the nine defendants who had pled guilty in this case. The sentences assigned to these men also varied considerably, but in each case the fine was in alternative to, rather than in addition to, imprisonment. Robert H. Swayne, in spite of earlier indications that he would be given special consideration, was sentenced to one year in jail or a fine of $10,000. C. D. Bunker was given the same sentence. The Flood brothers, James and George, who had chartered the *Olson & Mahony*, each received a year in jail or a $5,000 fine. Hengstler received a $3,000 fine, while Henry Kaufmann of the German consulate was fined $2,000. Theodore A. Anderson, captain of the *Sacramento*, about whom little had appeared in newspaper accounts and prosecution correspondence, was sentenced to six months in jail or a $1,000 fine. The corporate fines were mere slaps on the wrist, with $100 each being assessed against C. D. Bunker & Company, Northern and Southern Steamship Company, and Golden Gate Transport Company.

Because they had chosen not to plead guilty but were nevertheless found guilty by trial, Capelle and Bley were sentenced separately on January 3, 1919. Capelle was given 21 months at the McNeil Island federal penitentiary, and Bley was sentenced to 18 months confinement at the same facility.

An idealist may have been dissatisfied with the pragmatic nature of the sentencing, but something close to justice had been attained. Only a few key players had not been charged in any of the cases, chief among whom was John B. Starr-Hunt whose testimony in the *Maverick* case had been valuable to the prosecution. Charges against the customs house broker Marcos Martinez, the attorney Ray Howard, the transfer man Walter C. Hughes who was the San Diego consignee of the arms shipment, and the wealthy investor Leopold Michels, all of whom played roles in the acquisition of the *Annie Larsen* and *Maverick*, were dismissed.

Although initially the prosecutors had been worried about their ability to gain convictions on some of the defendants, under the circumstances in which the jurors in the Hindu case retired to deliberate the prosecutors quite possibly could have gained convictions over additional people who were only peripherally involved. A list of such people might include Captain Kessel of the *Maverick* and Captain Schluter of the *Annie Larsen*; Koeppel, the German consul in San Diego, who participated in the purchase of the *Larsen*; and A. V. Kirchheisen, the German agent who apparently was detained in Copenhagen in the summer of 1917 after the United States had entered the war, and was reportedly now held in Denver.

A few of the people involved in the conspiracies who were not prosecuted in any of the California cases were eventually picked up in prosecutions elsewhere. For example, Hans Tauscher who shipped the arms to the *Annie Larsen* in San Diego was prosecuted in a New York case, along with such important German diplomats as Franz von Papen and Wolf von Igel.[17] Similarly, H. L. Gupta, the Indian who was involved in the same transaction, was prosecuted in another New York case,[18] and Albert H. Wehde and George P. Boehm of the *Henry S.* incident in the Philippines were given extremely stiff sentences in still another case.[19]

No significant appeals to the verdicts were made by the defense. For the German nationals who were involved, serving time in a federal facility for a criminal conviction probably represented a gentler form of confinement than these men would have received if arrested as enemy aliens. Among the Americans, no one other than Bley and Capelle received a mandated sentence in excess of one year in prison, and the fines were moderate enough that these generally affluent men could handle them without financial ruin. Thus, a sense of fairness prevailed.

One of the goals of the prosecutors had been to recoup as much in the way of the cost of the trials as possible. Although no final accounting of these negotiations has been found, U. S. Attorney John W. Preston offered a financial deal to Robert Swayne, seeking to recover the excess profit that Northern and Southern Steamship Company had made on the sale of the *Sacramento*. This money, of course, should have been returned to the Germans who bought the ship with their funds, but Swayne and his fellow owners of the bogus company had pocketed the money, knowing that the Germans would not wish to go to court to recover it.

Preston's proposal to Swayne was that if the federal government were to libel the company for the amount at issue, $350,000, and the steamship company were to pay into the treasury of the United States this amount, then a fine for Swayne would be all that was necessary in achieving the ends of justice. Swayne countered with an offer of $250,000, but Preston felt confident that the other $100,000 would eventually be forthcoming. He was later proven wrong. In December, 1918, after the *Sacramento* case had been settled including additional jail time for Swayne, the federal government filed a libel against the Northern and Southern Steamship Company for $240,000.[20] It is not even clear whether this reduced amount was ever recovered.

Preston had previously told the Attorney General that with the $350,000 that his deal with Swayne could generate, plus another $50,000 in fines from the other defendants, the treasury would have recouped $400,000 in income from the prosecutions.[21] He did not mention the fact that the trials were estimated to have cost the government three million dollars.

In the final analysis, however, the trials quite possible had been worth the effort and expense. The federal government had taken the position, and had made it stick, that those who had profited unduly from the acts of the conspiracies and had remained unrepentant would now have to settle up or go to prison. This approach seemed like an eminently fair resolution of the lengthy and complex case.

CHAPTER TWELVE

OUTCOMES AND EFFECTS

Aside from their direct impact on defendants, trials of notorious cases have a way of producing results that represent good copy for newspapers, but little in the way of significant progress toward a better society. The German-Hindu Conspiracy cases of World War One would have to be regarded in this light.

Certainly, the ambiguities in neutrality law remained essentially unresolved after the trials. Fortunately, however, neutrality was no longer a national goal for the balance of World War One, nor for many years thereafter. The subsequent neutrality of 1939-41 quickly became a partisan neutrality, to the degree that the policy which the United States had tried so awkwardly to pursue during 1914-17 became, in time, an historical curiosity which it remains today.

Lacking a basis for comparison, it is difficult to assess whether, as a result of the events in the Pacific during the war, the response time and the corrective actions of the U. S. Navy, Department of State, and the Department of Justice improved in dealing with international challenges to neutrality. Perhaps, in time the leaders of those branches of government did become less inclined to accept at face value the explanations of foreign nations, although the nation's naiveté toward Japan in 1941 seems to suggest not.

As one might expect, American attitudes toward other nationalities changed as the war progressed. Germans in particular felt the wrath of public opinion. On the other hand, the British and French, now that they were allies of the United States, were treated with considerable newfound deference. Several instances of rather arrogant British internment of American vessels were overlooked, at the same time that the prosecution of the Hindu conspirators, which was a British goal with no real benefit for Americans, was pursued aggressively.

The morality, or lack thereof, of the behavior of the participants in the cargo conspiracies was never much of an issue. Consequently, during the post-war years when the public wanted to remember only the heroes of the war, such men as Sergeant York and Captain Rickenbacker, there was little thought given to any further punishment of those whose conduct had been adjudged treasonous. The political protesters of that era from such groups as the I. W. W. and the

Socialist Party were soon released, and the country entered into its era of "normalcy" with little desire to punish further the dissenters, slackers, and disloyal citizens of the war era.

Corporate offenders had similar treatment; in fact, some of the companies that were a part of the conspiracies seemed to have benefitted rather than suffered from their wartime activities. Swayne & Hoyt emerged as a much larger steamship company after the war, and soon was operating for the government several large transport/passenger vessels built by the U. S. Shipping Board, particularly the "502" class including the *Wolverine State* which went on under the aegis of the Dollar Line to be the *President Harrison*, the first of the round-the-world American passenger ships. Similarly, Olson & Mahony continued for a number of years in the steam schooner trade along the California coast, undaunted by any stigma acquired during the cargo conspiracies.

Furthermore, the principals of those firms, even those who went to prison and/or paid fines, were not unduly stigmatized by their actions. Although it has been impossible to follow up on most of these individuals, perhaps the aftermath for this group can be epitomized in the fate of its best known member, Robert Swayne. When this man died in 1935, his glowing obituary in a shipping journal made no mention of his involvement in the World War One cases.[1] Individual American mariners were also relatively unharmed by their roles in serving German interests during the war. Captains Anderson of the *Sacramento*, Paulsen of the *Mazatlan*, Schluter of the *Annie Larsen*, and Kessel of the *Maverick* all seemed to have resumed their careers with no great difficulty. In fact, Schluter briefly enjoyed public accolades in 1927 when he served as navigator for Martin Jensen who flew the airplane *Aloha* to a second-place finish in the Oakland to Honolulu "Dole Derby" race.[2]

The fate of two of the German mariners has been reported definitively. Captain Herman Othmer, supercargo aboard the *Larsen*, died in the loss of the U-99 in the North Sea.[3] The celebrated Fred Jebsen met a similar fate. Within a few weeks after joining the U-36 as a junior officer, he was lost when that submarine engaged in surface action with a small vessel which turned out to be a decoy, a British Q-boat which sank her attacker.[4] However, in spite of a number of well-documented reports of Jebsen's death in this incident, some American officials, particularly Preston of the Department of Justice, continued to believe that this German officer had escaped and remained alive, an evil legend that had not died.[5]

Although their careers were harder to follow than those of the American members of the cargo conspiracies, even the German diplomats demonstrated the ability to land on their feet. Two in particular would continue to be noticed by Americans. Von Papen, the military attaché at the Embassy, went on to play an important role in German affairs of state before and during World War Two. Von Brincken of the German consulate in San Francisco, who in 1919 had confessed to German complicity in many acts of sabotage as well as the cargo conspiracies, also played a number of colorful post-war roles; he stayed in the United States, and built a successful career as a character actor in Hollywood, including an appearance in *Hell's Angels* as Baron von Richtofen.[6]

Of the original group of six ships which were utilized by the conspirators, apparently only one, the *Maverick*, was lost while so engaged, although her final fate remains a mystery. Her collaborator, the *Annie Larsen*, as noted previously, was lost while engaged in peaceful pursuits late in the war. All the other ships directly involved in the story had remarkably long careers. The *Olson & Mahony* of 1907 went to the Gulf of California as the *Providencia* for a French copper mining firm; after the war her owners sent her to France where she worked out of Bordeaux until early in World War Two. The *Sacramento* had a long career under half a dozen other names until she was scrapped in the early 1930s. The *Marie* became the *Perene* for the Peruvian government steamship company after World War One, and was last listed in *Lloyds* in 1955 at the age of 50. The *Mazatlan* survived to a ripe old age as the *Edna*, dropping out of the registers in 1939 at the age of 36.

Among the four other American-flag vessels which were peripherally involved in the conspiracies, the steamer *Rio Pasig* was the only one to pay any price for her indiscretions. After being interned by the British in the Philippines early in the war for attempting to run coal to the Germans, she had disappeared in 1916 en route from Seattle to Vladivostock, an event that generated the rather unusual speculation that she had been torpedoed, even though German submarines had never been authoritatively located in the Pacific. The other steamer, the

Minnesotan, which had dispensed coal to German colliers in the Straits of Magellan, resumed her career for the American Hawaiian Steamship Company and was last listed in ship registers in 1939.

Although she remained in ship registers for several more years, little is known about the further service of the schooner *Henry S.* which had tried to mount a filibustering expedition to China from the Philippines. The other schooner, the *Alexander Agassiz,* which went raiding on the Mexican coast was lost in a grounding on the California coast not long after the war.[7]

Many loose ends remain in the story of the San Francisco conspiracies, but society seems to have recognized neither the need nor the desire to pursue these matters further. Viewed in retrospect, the whole episode now seems like a grade B movie, with grainy black and white pictures, stilted dialogue on a scratchy sound track, and an implausible plot made no more credulous by a series of stereotyped performances. Perhaps, however, that is exactly the way that the entire World War One experience is now perceived by the public.

If the early days of that war represented the final period in which the belligerents chivalrously played by the rules of civilized warfare, perhaps the shipping conspiracies of that era also marked the last of the 20th century international intrigues which were free from violence, treachery, dishonor, and, at times, even malice. As the war progressed, it was to be expected that men of honor would increasingly vanish from the scene among civilian conspirators, just as among military combatants. Consequently, the San Francisco shipping conspiracies, with their casts of essentially benign miscreants, had already become a series of anachronisms before they were ever resolved in the courtroom.

Under these circumstances, one is drawn toward the conclusion that these curious events of World War One on the Pacific Coast, with their vestigial links to an earlier era of genteel diplomacy as well as to a time of unbridled free enterprise, were unique one-time phenomena. Consequently, we will probably never again witness the unsettling spectacle of American shipping men using shadowy ships and cargoes in pursuit of personal goals which were contrary to the national interest, itself an ill-defined and transitory goal.

By the same token, however, we may never again encounter such an inherently interesting juxtaposition of people, loyalties, and responsibilities. The German purser who told an American captain how to run his ship, the janitor who owned a steamship company but did not operate it, the American naval officer who procured a gun-running schooner for a rebellion overseas, the fearless German officer who worried about getting picked up on a morals charge, the secretary who financed a ship acquisition with a bundle of cash dug out of a muff—the list of ironies and incongruities is endless. The prospect of never again encountering conspirators such as these is disheartening. Clearly, without these colorful people the World War One shipping conspiracies would have been no fun at all.

NOTES

Chapter One

1. Mark Sullivan, *Our Times, 1900-1925*, Volume V, *Over Here, 1914-1918*. New York: Charles Scribner's Sons, 1933, p. 52.
2. A useful discussion of the various rules of neutrality appears in J. W. Hall, *The Law of Naval Warfare*. London: Chapman & Hall, Ltd., 1921.
3. The explanation of the organization of naval forces in the Pacific is derived from Robert Erwin Johnson, *Thence Round Cape Horn: The Story of United States Naval Forces on Pacific Station, 1818-1923*. Annapolis, MD: Naval Institute Press, 1963.

Chapter Two

1. John Philips Cranwell, *Spoilers of the Sea, Wartime Raiders in the Age of Steam*. Freeport, NY: Books for Libraries Press, 1970, p. 150.
2. These attitudes toward coastal defense are described in David H. Grover, "America's Other Mine Force," *Sea Classics*, October, 1993, pp. 64-70.
3. *New York Times*, June 22, 1916, p. 2.
4. Villa's statement was reported in State Department Decimal File 862.20212/77, quoted in Barbara W. Tuchman, *The Zimmermann Telegram*. New York: Dell Publishing, 1958, p. 167.
5. The first of these attempts is described in a letter from Joseph H. Choate, American Ambassador to England, to Secretary of State John Hay, undated but apparently 1903, in the Hay Collection, Library of Congress. The second attempt is cited in a letter from Frederick H. Allen to Secretary of State Charles Evans Hughes, May 2, 1923, in State Department Decimal File 894.20214/283.
6. Much of the information on the movements of the *Leipzig* is from Harold D. Huycke, *To Santa Rosalia, Further and Back*. Newport News, VA: Mariners Museum, 1970. Captain Huycke cites as the source of the cruiser's movements, Erich Raeder, *Der Krieg zur See, 1914-1918*, Volume I, *Der Kreuzerkrieg in den Auschländischen Gewässern*. Berlin: Marine Archives, German Navy, 1922. This publication has been consulted, as has an English-language translation microfilmed by the National Archives.
7. Details of the messages and the departure of the cruisers appear in F. L. Oliver, "Two Code Messages," *Naval Institute Proceedings*, January, 1928, pp. 16-19.
8. *Ibid.*
9. Raeder, *op. cit.*, p. 349; also in translation, *op. cit.*, p. 430.
10. The 1914 evacuation was described in *Sunset* Magazine, July, 1914, pp. 145-51; also in *New York Times*, May 18, 1914, p. 3, and San Francisco *Chronicle*, May 18, 1914, p. 1. The detainment of the *Cetriana* in 1915 during another evacuation is reported in *New York Times*, April 30, 1915, p. 7.
11. The movements of the ship along the coast are recorded in Raeder, *op. cit.*, and in the translation, *op. cit.*

146

12. Letter, Supervisor, 12th Naval District, to Secretary of Navy, August 14, 1914, in RG 118.

13. Letter, Supervisor, 12th Naval District, to Secretary of the Navy, August 13, 1914, in RG 118.

14. Raeder, translation, *op. cit.*, p. 439.

15. *Ibid.*, pp. 439-40.

16. San Francisco *Chronicle*, August 22, 1914, p. 3.

17. Los Angeles *Times*, August 10, 1914, p. 1.

18. Los Angeles *Times*, August 17, 1914, p. 2.

19. Los Angeles *Times*, August 14, 1914, p. 1.

Chapter Three

1. The background of the German diplomatic and espionage networks can be found in Henry Landau, *The Enemy Within: The Inside Story of German Sabotage in America.* New York: G. P. Putnam's Sons, 1937. Also useful are John Price Jones and Paul Merrick Hollister, *The German Secret Service in America, 1914, 1918.* Boston: Small, Maynard & Co., 1918; and Earl E. Sperry, *German Plots and Intrigues in the United States During the Period of Our Neutrality.* Washington, DC: Committee on Public Information, Red, White, and Blue Series, No. 10, July, 1918.

2. Landau, *op. cit.*, p. 4.

3. John Walter, *German Surface Raiders in World War One.* Annapolis, MD: Naval Institute Press, 1994, p. 35.

4. San Francisco *Examiner*, August 3, 1914, p. 4.

Chapter Four

1. Various sources report that the *Mazatlan* had been registered under the Norwegian and/or German flags, and even the American flag, before becoming a Mexican-flag vessel. She apparently had been chartered by the U. S. government to bring refugees out of Mexico, which may account for the belief that she was registered American. The movements of the ship and those of the *Leipzig* are described in Huycke, *op. cit.*, as well as in newspaper accounts and in the translation of the Raeder history.

2. Letter, William G. McAdoo to Robert Lansing, August 20, 1914, in State Department Decimal File 763.72111/54.

3. *New York Times*, August 22, 1914, p. 5.

4. Letter, Robert Lansing to William G. McAdoo, August 22, 1914, in State Department Decimal File 763.72111/54.

5. Letter, Collector of Customs Davis, San Francisco, to William G. McAdoo, October 10, 1914, in State Department Decimal File 763.72111/446. The consignee in Guaymas was apparently W. Iberri & Sons, although some sources name F. G. Brale or Braue, a commission merchant in that port. It is more likely that this man was the consignor of the cargo.

6. This may have been true, although the trip to Guaymas had been advertised in the shipping papers as including a stop at San Pedro, and the ship loaded cargo there.

7. San Francisco *Bulletin*, October 5, 1914, p. 1, 2.

8. Details of the *Mazatlan's* trip to Guaymas were provided in the statement by Captain R. J. Paulsen, December 28, 1917, Seattle, Washington, in RG 118.

9. John B. Starr-Hunt statement, statement to Singapore Police, May 8-16, 1916, in RG 118.

10. 243 *Federal Reporter* 420.

11. Raeder, translation, *op. cit.*, p. 94.

12. *Ibid.*, p. 442.

13. Huycke, *op. cit.*, pp. 135-36.

14. *Ibid.*, pp. 148-50.

15. *Ibid.*, pp. 136-139.

16. Raeder, translation, *op. cit.*, p. 444.

17. San Francisco *Chronicle*, September 25, 1914, p. 14; San Francisco *Chronicle*, September 19, 1914, p. 12.

18. Huycke, *op. cit.*, p. 137.

19. *British Merchant Shipping (Losses), World War I*. Wellington, New Zealand: Ship and Marine Society, 1966, p. 1.

20. Letter, Dwight R. Messimer to the author, April 16, 1994. Messimer indicates that a tanker named *Elsinora* was under the control of the German *Etappe* in San Francisco. He cites as his source; Dieter Jung, Martin Mass, and Berndt Wenzel, *Tanker und Versorger der Deutchen Flotte, 1900-1980*. Stuttgart: Motorbuch Berlag, 1981. However, the author's recent research here and queries in England have been unable to verify a relationship between this ship and the *Etappen*.

21. Details of the battle are in many sources. Particularly useful is Thomas G. Frothingham, *The Naval History of the World War*, Volume I, *Offensive Operations, 1914-15*. Cambridge, MA: Harvard University Press, 1925.

22. Raeder, translation, *op. cit.*, pp. 450-51.

23. Huycke, *op. cit.*, p. 279.

24. The sequence of events in the detainment of the ship is described in the shipping columns of the San Diego *Union*, January 22, 1915, January 31, 1915, July 1, 1915, July 23, 1915.

25. *American Maritime Cases*, 1923, Volume II. Baltimore, MD: The Maritime Law Association of the United States, 1923, p. 955.

26. Aubrey Drury, researcher, "John Albert Hooper," *California Historical Society Quarterly*, Volume 31, 1952, p. 297. This account describes the business career of a San Francisco banker who frequently invested in ships, including the *Mazatlan*.

27. Letter, Cecil Spring Rice to Robert Lansing, October 24, 1914, in State Department Decimal File 763.72111/564. The coal company was generally identified in this correspondence by the name Moore, but the actual owners were apparently a pair of brothers, John and Julius

Rothschild, who figured prominently in the legal aftermath of this and other coal shipments.

28. Letter, Robert Lansing to Cecil Spring Rice, October 27, 1914, in State Department Decimal File 763.72111/564.

29. San Francisco *Bulletin*, October 5, 1914, p. 1, 2.

30. Letter, French Ambassador Jusserand to the Secretary of State, September 21, 1914; letter, Secretary of State to the French Ambassador, September 29, 1914, both in State Department Decimal File 763.72111/204.

31. Raeder, translation, *op. cit.*, p. 154.

32. Letter, Robert Lansing to Cecil Spring Rice, October 27, 1914, in State Department Decimal File 763.72111/564. The Raeder translation suggests that a second ship was similarly seized in the Gulf of California and taken to British Columbia for internment.

33. *New York Times*, November 21, 1914, p. 7, quoting Captain Robert Israel of the seagoing launch *Nonsuch* who witnessed the coaling.

34. Los Angeles *Times*, April 14, 1915, p. 1.

35. *New York Times*, April 14, 1915, p. 8.

36. Gordon Newell, editor, *The H. S. McCurdy Marine History of the Northwest*. Seattle: Superior Publishing Company, 1966, p. 266.

Chapter Five

1. Raeder, *op. cit.*, p. 345.

2. Letter, German Ambassador to the Secretary of State, October 14, 1914, in State Department Decimal File 195.1/128.

3. *The Guide*, September 26, 1914.

4. *The Register*, August 12, 1914.

5. On the matter of cargo, the Raeder translation quotes Dr. Reimer, supply officer of the *Leipzig*, who went aboard the *Alexandria* off Cape San Lucas for the balance of the trip into San Francisco.

6. Seattle *Times*, July 27, 1914, p. 8.

7. San Francisco *Chronicle*, August 8, 1914, p. 15.

8. *Ibid.*

9. Raeder, translation, *op. cit.*, p. 345.

10. San Francisco *Chronicle*, August 8, 1914, p. 5.

11. San Francisco *Chronicle*, December 18, 1918, p. 9.

12. Letter, U. S. District Attorney John W. Preston to F. H. Duehay, President, U. S. Board of Parole, January 25, 1919, in RG 118.

13. *Ibid.*

14. San Francisco *Chronicle*, September 23, 1914, p. 13.

15. Letter, Secretary of State to the German Ambassador, December 10, 1914, in State Department Decimal File 195.1/160.

16. Invoice of Rolph Navigation & Coal Company to C. D. Bunker & Company, September 10, 1914, in RG 118.

17. Preston to Duehay, *op. cit.*

18. German Ambassador to Secretary of State, *op. cit.*

19. British Consul General at San Francisco to British Ambassador, October 10, 1914, in State Department Decimal File 195.1/142.

20. Walter Macarthur, "Voyage of the *Sacramento*," Naval Institute *Proceedings*, August, 1934, p. 1062.

21. Cited in *New York Times*, September 25, 1914, p. 6.

22. *New York Times*, November 11, 1914, p. 14.

23. *New York Times*, September 25, 1914, p. 8.

24. Statement of Peter Madison, First Assistant Engineer, SS *Sacramento*, in RG 118.

25. Macarthur, *op. cit.*

26. San Francisco *Chronicle*, October 9, 1914, p. 4.

27. Information about the crew is from the original shipping articles and crew list, in RG 118.

28. *Ibid.*

29. *Ibid.*

30. Original crew list signed by Captain T. A. Anderson, October 14, 1914, in RG 118.

31. Statements of Benjamin F. Tracey and Peter Madison, engineering officers of the SS *Sacramento*, in RG 118.

32. Macarthur, *op. cit.*

33. Explanations of these arrangements are in the statements of the two engineers, and in Macarthur, *op. cit.*

34. Tracey, *op. cit.*

35. William Kooiman, *The Grace Ships, 1869-1969*. Point Reyes: CA: Komar Publishing, 1990, pp. 267-68.

36. Madison, *op. cit.*

37. This information is from the shipping articles.

38. Chief Mate's Log, SS *Sacramento*, for indicated dates, in RG 118.

39. San Francisco *Chronicle*, October 16, 1914, p. 14.

40. Madison, *op. cit.*

41. *Ibid.*

42. San Francisco *Chronicle*, October 16, 1914, p. 14.

Chapter Six

1. Copies of both sets of the logbook are contained in Folder II, Box 19, Record Group 118, Records of the U. S. Attorney, San Francisco, at the Pacific Sierra Branch, National Archives, San Bruno, California.

2. Statements of the engineers, *op. cit.*

3. Madison, *op. cit.*

4. *Ibid.*

5. The texts of the radio messages sent by and to the Sacramento were supplied by the American consul at Valparaiso who found copies on a table in a stateroom on the ship.

6. The Germans spelled the name of the island as three words, similar to Mas a Tierra, the other island in the Juan Fernandez group. Chile spelled the name as two words, Mas Afuera.

7. Statements of the engineers, *op. cit.*

8. Differences of opinion exist as to the fate of the *Valentine*. E. Keble Chatterton in *The Sea Raiders* asserts that the *Leipzig* sank the vessel the day after the Battle of Coronel, but the extensive Chilean claim against Germany for violation of her neutrality places the *Valentine* at Mas Afuera under German control, but indicates that no eye-witnesses to her sinking could be located. When last seen, she had lost two masts, but was still anchored at the island.

9. Letter, Kosmos Line Agency, Valparaiso, to Harold H. Ebey, December 2, 1914, in RG 118.

10. Letter, Secretary of State to German Ambassador, December 10, 1914, in State Department Decimal File 195.1/160.

11. Telegram, Ambassador in Chile to Secretary of State, December 29, 1914, in State Department Decimal File 763.72111Sa1/12.

12. Telegram, Secretary of State to Ambassador in Chile, December 30, 1914, in State Department Decimal File 763.72111Sa1/12.

13. San Francisco *Chronicle*, June 10, 1914, p. 23.

14. Balance Sheet, Northern and Southern Steamship Company, August 5, 1918, in RG 118.

Chapter Seven

1. Jack McNairn and Jerry MacMullen, *Ships of the Redwood Coast*. Stanford, CA: Stanford University Press, 1945, p. 62.

2. Letter British Ambassador to Secretary of State, November 23, 1914, in State Department Decimal File 763.72111/736.

3. Letter, Secretary of State to the German Ambassador, December 10, 1914, in State Department Decimal File 195.1/160.

4. Letter, Secretary of State to the British Embassy, December 16, 1914, in State Department Decimal File 763.72111/1106.

5. Letter, Secretary of State to the British Ambassador, November 25, 1914, in State Department Decimal File 763.72111/736.

6. Much of the information about the conspiracy and the conspirators is from the letter of U. S. Attorney John W. Preston to the United States Parole Board, *op. cit.*

7. *Ibid.*

8. *Ibid.*

9. San Francisco *Chronicle*, November 25, 1914, p. 5.

10. San Francisco *Chronicle*, December 2, 1915, p. 1.

11. San Francisco *Examiner*, December 3, 1914, p. 3; December 4, 1914, p. 3.

12. San Francisco *Chronicle*, December 2, 1914, p. 4.

13. Letter, Preston to Board of Parole, *op. cit.*

14. San Francisco *Examiner*, November 2, 1915, p. 5.

15. Leopold Michels, President of Greenbaum, Michels, & Co., quoted in San Francisco *Examiner*, December 25, 1914, p. 6.

16. San Francisco *Examiner*, November 28, 1914, p. 3.

17. San Francisco *Examiner*, December 2, 1914, p. 3.

18. The travels of the *Olson & Mahony* and the *Oliver J. Olson* for this period are documented in the daily San Francisco shipping journal, *The Guide.*

19. San Francisco *Examiner*, January 5, 1915, p. 3. The claim was for the loss of 16 days charter at $210, plus the loss of outbound and return freight receipts and a general loss.

20. San Francisco *Examiner*, March 2, 1915, p. 5.

Chapter Eight

1. A good short summary of the German-Hindu cases appears in Jones and Hollister, *op. cit.*

2. Letter, Assistant U. S. Attorney Robert O'Connor, San Francisco, to United States Attorney, Seattle, July 9, 1915, in RG 118.

3. "Memorandum on the Indian Activities in This Country," initialed CMS and believed to be Charles M. Storey of the Department of Justice, Washington, D. C., July 1, 1916, in RG 118.

4. Testimony of John B. Starr-Hunt, summary of the trial transcript p. 3778, in RG 118.

5. Hizar's role is explained through various witnesses in summary of trial testimony. His own explanations are on p. 4378 of the transcript summary in RG 118.

6. Landau, *op. cit.*, p. 30.

7. Coded cable 449, Foreign Minister Zimmermann to Ambassador von Bernstorff, quoted in Landau, *ibid.*, p. 29-30.

8. Harish K. Puri, *Ghadar Movement: Ideology, Organisation, & Strategy.* N. P.: Guru Nahak Dev University Press, 1983, p. 91.

9. Memorandum for "Warren," undated and March 21, 1916, initialed CMS, in RG 118.

10. Letter, Assistant U. S. Attorney Robert O'Connor, San Francisco, to U. S. Attorney, Seattle, July 6, 1915, in RG 118. However, a story datelined San Diego in the Los Angeles *Times*, January 15, 1915, p. 2, suggested that both sides in the revolution believed that the guns were headed for Carranza forces: "The Villa gunboat *Korrigan II* and the Carranza gunboat *Guerrero* are making their way up the coast of lower California to a rendezvous off Coronado Islands, according to the Mexican secret service here today. The mission of the *Korrigan II*, it was reported, is to confiscate the rifles and ammunition and to sink the *Annie Larsen*, while that of the *Guerrero* is to save the schooner and sink the *Korrigan*."

11. Policies, or perhaps more accurately, enforcement of policies, regarding the export of arms to Mexico changed from time to time. In August, 1915, six months after the *Annie Larsen* had encountered no trouble in taking a shipload of arms destined for Topolobampo, the British steamer *Prince Albert*, under charter to Southwestern Steamship Company with a cargo of arms to Mazatlan, was denied clearance at San Pedro, forcing the unloading of the weapons. San Francisco *Call-Bulletin*, August 14, 1915, p. 2.

12. Memorandum to Warren, undated, *op. cit.*

152

13. San Francisco *Examiner*, January 31, 1918, p. 1.
14. Letter, O'Connor to U. S. Attorney, Seattle, July 6, 1915, *op. cit.*
15. Letter, Assistant U. S. Attorney Robert O'Connor to U. S. Attorney, Seattle, July 9, 1915, in RG 118.
16. Letter, O'Connor to U. S. Attorney, Seattle, July 6, 1915, *op. cit.*
17. Memorandum to Warren, undated, *op. cit.*
18. Report of interview between federal agent E. M. Blumford and crew member Peter Olsen, San Francisco, November 24, 1917, in RG 118.
19. Memorandum to Warren, March 21, 1916, *op. cit.*
20. Starr-Hunt, statement, *op. cit.*
21. Olsen interview, *op. cit.*
22. Diary of Commander Raymond D. Hasbrouck, USN, former commanding officer of USS *Yorktown*, for April 26-27, 1915, abstracted in report of federal agent C. B. Treadway, September 24, 1917, in RG 118.
23. Olsen interview, *op. cit.*
24. San Francisco *Bulletin*, January 12, 1918, p. 8.
25. Such a statute remains on the books today in the form of 18 USC 960.
26. Letter, H. Othmer to Fregattenkapitän Toussaint, January 14, 1916, in Mossman papers.
27. San Francisco *Examiner*, September 17, 1916, p. 29.
28. Jones and Hollister, *op. cit.*, p. 265.
29. San Francisco *Chronicle*, March 21, 1917, p. 2.
30. Naval Institute *Proceedings*, May 17, 1917, p. 1079, quoting New York *Herald*, April 7, 1917.
31. Seattle *Times*, November 17, 1918, p. 30.

Chapter Nine

1. Testimony of Harry J. Hart, shipbroker, transcript summary, p. 5492.
2. Testimony of Gustave N. Koeppel, German consular agent in San Diego, transcript summary, p. 1657.
3. *Ibid.*, p. 1631.
4. Testimony of A. A. Moran, steamship executive, transcript summary, p. 3490.
5. Hart, *op. cit.*
6. Testimony of J. C. Rohlfs of Standard Oil, transcript summary, p. 2561; testimony of J. F. Craig, shipyard owner, transcript summary, p. 5270.
7. Testimony of Fred R. Cooper of Standard Oil, transcript summary, p. 2526.
8. Rohlfs, *op. cit.*, p. 3792.
9. Craig, *op. cit.*, p. 5301.
10. Testimony of Ray Howard, attorney, transcript summary, p. 2579.
11. San Francisco *Examiner*, January 24, 1918, p. 5.
12. "Memo of Names to be Submitted to Grand Jury," Box 4, Folder 5, RG 118.

13. Howard, *op. cit.*, p. 2580.

14. Letter, Special Agent Don S. Rathbun, San Francisco, to Special Agent E. M. Blanford, Los Angeles, June 8, 1917, in RG 118.

15. Memorandum to Warren, March 21, 1916, *op. cit.* All the correspondence among federal agents refers to this man as "a Mr. Smith," as if his first name were unknown, which is unlikely if an actual charter document existed. The man's initials appear in a story in the San Francisco *Chronicle*, January 24, 1918, p. 9.

16. Statement of Harry J. Potoff, union official, San Pedro, November 21, 1917, in RG 118.

17. Starr-Hunt, statement, *op. cit.*

18. Potoff, *op. cit.*

19. Starr-Hunt, statement, *op. cit.*

20. Crew list of the *Maverick*, *op. cit.*

21. Statement of William J. P. Kessel before Assistant U. S. Attorney Adams, San Francisco, July 3, 1918, in RG 118.

22. Starr-Hunt, statement, *op. cit.*

23. *Ibid.*

24. Statement of J. C. Rudbach, ship chandler, San Pedro, November 22, 1917, in RG 118.

25. Starr-Hunt, statement, *op. cit.*

26. *Ibid.*

27. *Ibid.*

28. Letter, W. D. Prideaux, Master, USS *Nanshan*, to Commander-in-Chief, Pacific Fleet, May 13, 1915, in RG 118.

29. *Ibid.*

30. Starr-Hunt, statement, *op. cit.*

31. *Ibid.*

32. *Ibid.*

33. *Ibid.*

34. Testimony of Sue Clark, secretary to Jebsen, transcript summary, p. 3477-79.

Chapter Ten

1. Eelbo's name appears in most documents as Elbo, but his clearly-legible signature on papers in RG 118 indicates that he spelled it with two e's.

2. This company had been one of the pioneer sugar-growing and trading companies in the islands. Its assets were appropriated by the federal government later in World War I, with the company eventually emerging as American Factors, an American corporation which ultimately became Amfac. See William L. Worden, *Cargoes: Matson's First Century in the Pacific*. Honolulu: University Press of Hawaii, 1981.

3. Starr-Hunt statement, *op. cit.* This document is the source of much of the information about the *Maverick*'s voyage to the Far East.

4. San Francisco *Examiner*, December 18, 1915, p. 5. The second officer of the *Maverick*, William Reed, who was one of nine crewmen who

had returned to San Francisco, was the source of the information about Starr-Hunt and Jebsen.

5. San Francisco *Chronicle*, March 7, 1916, p. 5..

6. Receipt to Jebsen, signed by H. C. Nelson, Master, Hilo, June 21, 1915, in RG 118.

7. Starr-Hunt statement, *op. cit.*

8. Memorandum for Assistant Attorney General Charles Warren, from Charles M. Storey, undated, in RG 118. It is interesting to recall that Peter Olsen of the *Larsen* crew claimed that, after failing to reach Socorro Island, the schooner had tried to reach an island at 172 degrees east longitude, roughly the location of the Marshall Islands.

9. *Ibid.* The San Blas mentioned here is an inland community in Sinaloa, not the port of the same name farther down the Mexican coast.

10. San Francisco *Examiner*, March 7, 1916, p. 5.

11. Memorandum, Charles M. Storey to Warren, March 21, 1916, in RG 118.

12. Letter, Chief of the Secret Service, Office of the Chief Commissioner, Police Department, Batavia, to Consul General of the Netherlands, San Francisco, November 21, 1915, in RG 118.

13. Starr-Hunt, statement, *op. cit.*

14. No complete account of the *Henry S.* incident has been found. Fragments of the story appear in various documents and correspondence in RG 118.

15. Puri, *op. cit.*, p. 95.

16. Giles T. Brown, "The Hindu Conspiracy, 1914-1917," *Pacific Historical Review*, Volume 17, 1948, pp. 307-08.

17. Statement, Carl Thorsen, in RG 118.

18. The dates of the ship's arrival in various ports and of her internment in Batavia are from *The Guide*, the daily shipping publication in San Francisco which presumably obtained the information from the standard sources of ship movement reports.

19. San Francisco *Chronicle*, December 18, 1915, p. 9.

20. *Ibid.*, p. 5.

21. Statement of William J. P. Kessel, in RG 118.

22. San Francisco *Chronicle*, December 18, 1915, p. 9.

23. San Francisco *Chronicle*, September 13, 1916, p. 5.

24. San Francisco *Examiner*, March 7, 1916, p. 5.

25. San Francisco *Examiner*, October 21, 1916, p. 1.

26. Puri, *op. cit.*, p. 92.

27. Anil Baran Ganguly, *Ghadar Revolution in America*. New Delhi: Metropolitan, 1980, p. 71, citing R. C. Mazumder, *History of the Freedom Movement in India*, pp. 436-44.

28. Letter, Harry J. Hart to William Kessel, September 20, 1916, in RG 118.

29. San Francisco *Chronicle*, September 26, 1916, p. 4.

30. *New York Times*, February 11, 1917, p. 4.

31. Letter, George MacGoldrick to Collector of Customs, Manila, August 9, 1917, in RG 118. Federal financial support for this transaction is mentioned in San Francisco *Chronicle*, December 13, 1917, p. 13.

32. MacGoldrick, *ibid.*

33. *Merchant Vessels of the United States*, Washington, DC, 1917.

34. This information is posted in a ledger of missing ships recorded a number of years ago, presumably from information at the San Francisco Marine Exchange, and preserved at the National Maritime Museum in San Francisco. This entry indicated that the ship was bound for "Cubu" which could be Cuba or Cebu in the Philippines. According to notices in the *Register*, a New York shipping publication, the destination was Cienfuegos in Cuba.

35. San Francisco *Chronicle*, December 13, 1917, p. 9, 13.

36. *New York Times*, October 4, 1917, p. 4, 24.

37. *Ibid.*

38. Details concerning this storm are from the weather records of the National Oceanographic and Atmospheric Administration in Silver Springs, Maryland, and from those of the Fleet Numerical Meteorology and Oceanography Detachment of the U. S. Navy at Asheville, North Carolina.

39. San Francisco *Chronicle*, December 13, 1917, p. 2.

40. *Ibid.*

41. San Francisco *Examiner*, December 13, 1917, p. 13.

Chapter Eleven

1. Much of the information about the day-to-day conduct of the trials is from San Francisco and Oakland newspapers.

2. This man may have been A. V. Kircheisen, the German spy known as K-17, who under the name of Phillips, with the first name reported variously as Charles or Thomas, had rented the car with which Page/Othmer escaped from the *Annie Larsen* at Hoquiam. However, that event was part of the German-Hindu Conspiracy, and not related to the earlier cargo conspiracies.

3. Curiously, one of the Indian "waiters" aboard the *Maverick* appears in the crew list as "J. Johansen."

4. Preston to the Attorney General, undated but from context late in 1918 prior to the conclusion of the trial for case 6133.

5. Oakland *Tribune*, April 30, 1918, p. 6.

6. Preston to the Attorney General, June 18, 1915.

7. Jones and Hollister, *op. cit.*, p. 282.

8. Landau, *op. cit.*, p. 33.

9. Emily C. Brown, *Har Dayal.* Tucson, AZ: University of Arizona Press, 1975, p. xii. Another researcher, James Mossman, reports that a copy of the transcript exists at the library of the University of British Columbia in Vancouver. Reportedly, ten copies of the 6000-page transcript were made.

10. Information on this case appears in RG 21, U. S. District Courts, National Archives, Pacific Southwest Branch, Laguna Niguel, CA.

11. San Francisco *Chronicle*, April 18, 1918, p. 1.

156

12. San Francisco *Examiner*, December 15, 1917, p. 11.

13. Oakland *Tribune*, April 30, 1918, p. 6.

14. Said Hengstler, "It is my honest desire and prayer that America will crush the military power of Germany, and that I will yet be able to do my man's share in bringing this about." Oakland *Tribune*, April 30, 1918, p. 6.

15. Transcript summary, p. 4596.

16. San Francisco *Examiner*, January 10, 1918, p. 5.

17. U. S. v. TAUSCHER et al. District Court, Southern District of New York, June 12, 1916. 223 *Federal Reporter* 597.

18. 244 *Federal Reporter* 287.

19. Jones and Hollister, *op. cit.*, p. 261.

20. San Francisco *Chronicle*, December 17, 1918, p. 6.

21. Letter, John W. Preston to Attorney General, undated but from context mid-1918, in RG 118.

Chapter Twelve

1. San Francisco *Chronicle*, August 17, 1927, p. 1. Sources differ widely on the outcome of this event. The *Encyclopedia Britannica* says that only three planes finished from the field of nine that started this race; the other six were lost at sea, along with the lives of ten people.

2. *Marine Digest*, August 15, 1936, p. 6.

3. *Ehrenrangliste der Kaiserlich Deutschen Marine, 1914-18*. Berlin: Thorman & Goetsch, 1930, p. 832.

4. *Ibid.*, p. 886; also in *Dur Krieg zur See*, Volume IV, *Der Krieg in der Nordsee*. Berlin: E. S. Mittler & Sons, 1924, p. 222.

5. Letter, John W. Preston to the Attorney General, December 24, 1918, in RG 118.

6. This information can be found in David Ragan, *Who's Who in Hollywood: The Largest Cast of International Film Personalities Ever Assembled*. New York and Oxford: Facts on File, 1992.

7. Newspaper clipping, from context 1921 but otherwise unidentified, in papers of William Reordan, son of the captain of the gunboat which had detained this vessel in 1918.

BIBLIOGRAPHY

BOOKS

American Maritime Cases, 1923, Volume II. Baltimore, MD: The Maritime Law Association of the United States, 1923.

Bennett, Geoffrey, *Coronel and the Falklands*. London: B. T. Batsford, Ltd., 1962.

British Merchant Shipping (Losses) World War I. Wellington: New Zealand Ship and Marine Society, 1966.

Brown, Emily C., *Har Dayal*. Tucson, AZ: University of Arizona Press, 1975.

Burdick, Charles, *The Frustrated Raider, The Story of the German Cruiser Cormoran in World War I*. Carbondale and Edwardsville, IL: Southern Illinois University Press, 1979.

Chatterton, E. Keble, *The Sea Raiders*. London: Hurst & Blackett, Ltd., 1931.

Conway's All the World's Fighting Ships, 1906-1921. London: Conway Maritime Press.

Corbett, Julian S., *History of the Great War, Naval Operations*, v. I. London: Longmans, Green & Co., 1920.

Cranwell, John Philips, *Spoilers of the Sea: Wartime Raiders in the Age of Steam*. Freeport, NY: Books for Libraries Press, 1970.

Dorwart, Jeffery M., *The Office of Naval Intelligence: The Birth of America's First Intelligence Agency, 1865-1918*. Annapolis, MD: Naval Institute Press, 1979.

Dupuy, Trevor Nevitt, *The Military History of World War I*, V. IX, *Naval and Overseas War, 1914-15*. New York: Franklin Watts, Inc., 1967.

Ehrenrangliste der Kaiserlich Deutschen Marine, 1914-18. Berlin: Thorman & Goetsch, 1930.

Ellis, Edward Robb, *Echoes of Distant Thunder: Life in the United States, 1914-1918*. New York: Coward, McCann & Geoghegan, Inc., 1975.

Frothingham, Thomas G., *The Naval History of the World War*, Volume I, *Offensive Operations, 1914-1915*. Cambridge, MA: Harvard University Press, 1925.

Ganguly, Anil Baran, *Ghadar Revolution in America*. New Delhi: Metropolitan, 1980.

Hall, J. W., *The Law of Naval Warfare*. London: Chapman & Hall, Ltd., 1921.

Haws, Duncan, *Merchant Fleets in Profile*, Volume Four, *The Ships of the Hamburg America, Adler and Carr Lines*. Cambridge, England: Patrick Stephens, 1980.

Hough, Richard A., *The Great War at Sea, 1914-1918*. New York: Oxford University Press, 1983.

Hoyt, Edwin P., *The Last Cruise of the Emden*. New York: The Macmillan Company, 1966.

———, *Raider Wolf, The Voyage of Captain Nerger 1916-1918*. New York: Paul S. Eriksson, 1974.

158

Huycke, Harold D., *To Santa Rosalia, Further and Back*. Newport News, VA: The Mariners Museum, 1970.

Janes Fighting Ships. London: Janes Fighting Ships, annual.

Johnson, Robert Erwin, *Thence Round Cape Horn, The Story of United States Naval Forces on Pacific Station, 1818-1923*. Annapolis, MD: United States Naval Institute, 1963.

Jones, John Price, and Hollister, Paul Merrick, *The German Secret Service in America, 1914-1918*. Boston: Small, Maynard & Co., 1918.

Jung, Dieter; Mass, Martin; and Wenzel, Berndt, *Tanker und Versorger der Deutschen Flotte, 1900-1980*. Stuttgart: Motorbuch Bulag, 1981.

Kooiman, William, *The Grace Ships, 1869-1969*. Point Reyes, CA: Komar Publishing, 1990.

Landau, Henry, *The Enemy Within*. New York: Putnam, 1937.

Marder, Arthur J., *From the Dreadnought to Scapa Flow*, Volume II, *The War Years: to the Eve of Jutland, 1914-1916*. New York: Oxford University Press, 1965.

Merchant Vessels of the United States. Washington, DC:, 1917.

McNairn, Jack, and MacMullen, Jerry, *Ships of the Redwood Coast*. Stanford, CA: Stanford University Press, 1945.

Navy Yearbook. Washington: Government Printing Office, 1914, 1918.

Newell, Gordon, editor, *The H. W. McCurdy Marine History of the Northwest*. Seattle, WA: Superior Publishing Company, 1959.

Oppenheim, L., *International Law*, V. II, *War and Neutrality*, 6th edition, edited by H. Lauterback. New York: Longmans, Green & Co., 1940.

Papers Relating to the Foreign Relations of the United States. Washington: Government Printing Office, 1905-1919.

Potter, E. B., editor, *Sea Power, A Naval History*. Englewood Cliffs, NJ: Prentice-Hall, Inc., 1960.

Puri, Harish K., *Ghadar Movement: Ideology, Organisation, & Strategy*. N. P.: Guru Nahak Dev University Press, 1983.

Raeder, Erich, *Der Krieg zur See, 1914-1918*, Volume I, *Der Kreuzerkrieg In Den Auslandischen Gewassern*. Berlin: Marine-Archive, 1922.

——, *Dur Krieg zur See*, Volume IV, *Der Krieg in der Nordsee*. Berlin: E. S. Mittler & Sons, 1924.

Ragan, David, *Who's Who in Hollywood: The Largest Cast of International Film Personalities Ever Assembled*. New York and Oxford: Facts on File, 1992.

Rocuant, Enrique, *The Neutrality of Chile: The Grounds that Prompted and Justified It*. Valparaiso: Sociedad Imprenta y Litografia Universo, 1919.

Scott, James Brown, editor, *The Hague Conventions and Declarations of 1899 and 1907*. New York: Oxford University Press, 1915.

Silverstone, Paul H., *U. S. Warships of World War I*. Garden City, NY: Doubleday & Co., 1970.

Sperry, Earl E., *German Plots and Intrigues in the United States During the Period of Our Neutrality*. Washington, DC: Committee on Public Information, Red, White, and Blue Series, No.; 10, July, 1918.

Sprout, Harold and Margaret, *The Rise of American Naval Power, 1776-1918*. Princeton, NJ: Princeton University Press, 1939.

Sullivan, Mark, *Our Times, 1900-1925*, Volume V, *Over Here, 1914-1918*. New York: Charles Scribner's Sons, 1933.
Sweetman, Jack, *American Naval History, An Illustrated Chronology*. Annapolis, MD: Naval Institute Press, 1984.
Thomas, Lowell, *Count Luckner, The Sea Devil*. New York: Garden City Publishing, 1927.
Tuchman, Barbara W., *The Zimmermann Telegram*. New York: Dell Publishing, 1958.
Walter, John, *The Kaiser's Pirates: German Surface Raiders in World War One*. Annapolis, MD: Naval Institute Press, 1994.
Worden, William L., *Cargoes: Matson's First Century in the Pacific*. Honolulu: University Press of Hawaii, 1981.

ARTICLES

Brown, Giles T., "The Hindu Conspiracy, 1914-1917," *Pacific Historical Review*, V. 17, 1948.
Drury, Aubrey, researcher, "John Albert Hooper," *California Historical Society Quarterly*, Volume 31, 1952.
Grover, David H., "America's Other Mine Force," *Sea Classics*, October, 1993.
Macarthur, Walter, "Voyage of the *Sacramento*," Naval Institute *Proceedings*, August, 1934.
Oliver, F. L., "Two Code Messages," Naval Institute *Proceedings*, January, 1938.
Wood, Chester C., "Background of Coronel and Falklands," Naval Institute *Proceedings*, July, 1934.

COLLECTED PAPERS

James Mossman
    Translations from German language sources, legal correspondence, etc.
William Reordan
    Correspondence relating to naval operations in the Gulf of California during 1917-18.

UNPUBLISHED SOURCES

Record Group 21, U. S. District Courts, National Archives. Laguna Niguel, California.
Record Group 59, State Department Decimal Files, National Archives, Washington, DC.
Record Group 118, U. S. Attorneys and Marshals, National Archives, San Bruno, California.
Weather Records of the National Oceanographic and Atmospheric Administration, Silver Springs, Maryland.
Weather Records of the U. S. Navy Fleet Numerical Meteorology and Oceanography Detachment, Ashville, North Carolina.

160

SHIP LOGS

SS *Sacramento*
USS *Yorktown*

NEWSPAPERS CITED

Los Angeles *Times*
New York *Herald*
New York Times
Oakland *Enquirer*
Oakland *Tribune*
San Diego *Union*
San Francisco *Call*
San Francisco *Bulletin*
San Francisco *Call-Bulletin*
San Francisco *Chronicle*
San Francisco *Examiner*
Seattle *Times*
Tacoma *Tribune*

SHIPPING PUBLICATIONS

The Guide, San Francisco
Marine Digest, Seattle
The Maritime Record, New York

INDEX

162

168

PICTURE CREDITS